EARLY FROST

EARLY FROST

THE FIRST THREE BOOKS

Robert Frost

Edited by Jeffrey Meyers

THE ECCO PRESS

THE ECCO PRESS
100 WEST BROAD STREET
HOPEWELL, NEW JERSEY 08525

Published simultaneously in Canada by
Penguin Books Canada Ltd., Ontario
Printed in the United States of America

LIBRARY OF CONGRESS CATALOGING-IN-PUBLICATION DATA

Early Frost : the first three books / edited by Jeffrey Meyers. — 1st ed.
p.   cm.
Includes index.
Contents: Introduction — A boy's will — North of Boston —
Mountain interval.
ISBN 0-88001-447-4 (paper)
1. Frost, Robert, 1874–1963.   I. Meyers, Jeffrey.
PS3511.R94A6   1996
811'.52—dc20   95-26679

Designed by Jonathan Greene
The text of this book is set in English Monotype Dante

9 8 7 6 5 4 3 2 1

FIRST EDITION

CONTENTS

Part II

Part III

NORTH OF BOSTON

MOUNTAIN INTERVAL

INTRODUCTION

ROBERT FROST published his first poem in 1894 and his first book, while living in England, in 1913. During his twenty-year struggle to achieve recognition, while he worked as a chicken farmer and a schoolteacher, Frost had ample time to develop his technique of literary allusion, his ideas about poetic diction, and his concept of the "sound of sense." In his first three books—*A Boy's Will, North of Boston,* and *Mountain Interval*—finally published between 1913 and 1916 in a surge of confidence and creativity, his poetic theories were fully realized.

"Poetry begins in reading of books," Frost declared, and the poet "writes out of the eddy in his mind of all the books he ever read. . . . The whole thing is performance and prowess and feats of association." The music of his verse, drifting through his head, set off associations of other poems he'd read, and the rich bequest of his predecessors directly inspired his own poetry. To be fully understood, Frost's poems must be read not only in the context of his life, and in relation to other poems in the entire body of his work, but also in the tradition of English poetry, which he devoured during his solitary years in rural New Hampshire. This devoted study was the most vital part of Frost's education.

Though their poetic practice was quite different, Frost had a great deal in common with his contemporary, T. S. Eliot. Just as Frost believed that "a poem is best read in the light of all the other poems ever written," so Eliot, in "Tradition and the Individual Talent," defined his own poetic method as well as the one Frost had adopted. It is extraordinary that while teaching in an obscure village, Frost discovered and practiced a method of composition that the high priest of modernism would also formulate in a more sophisticated way. Both believed that the poet belonged to a historical tradition, which provided a storehouse of images and ideas that the modern writer could use and build on.

Both Eliot and Frost drew extensively on other poets, ancient and modern. But while Eliot usually quoted directly, signaling his sources with quotation marks, foreign words, and footnotes, Frost subtly disguised and transformed his allusions—in his letters as well as in his poems. He did not give the reader intellectual pleasure through the shock of recognizing a familiar line in an unusual context, as Eliot did. But by subtly embedding quotations in his own text, Frost offered the reader the illusion that the whole new artifact, his poem, was familiar in a deeply satisfying way. "It's fun to quote something," he playfully said, "to make everybody wonder where you got that." Frost and Eliot were actually doing the same thing: re-possessing the poetry of the past by bringing it to bear on the present moment. Eliot liked to startle by juxtaposing contemporary scenes and images with touchstones from the literary tradition. Frost also used quotation for ironic contrast, but he more often transformed and renewed the source of his allusions. In the most sophisticated adaptations—like "After Apple-Picking"—he paid homage to the great poems he knew by heart, and let the mood of Keats's "Ode to a Nightingale" permeate and enhance his own very different work of art.

The classicist Helen Bacon observed that Frost's "direct allusions extend the sense and often give coherence and meaning to apparently incidental details, making the poem both more complex and more unified." The poetry that influenced and echoed through Frost's work was not, as with Eliot, from Dante, the Jacobean playwrights, the Metaphysicals, and the French Symbolists, but from the Bible, the Latin poets, the ballads, Shakespeare, the English Romantics, and the Victorians. Frost has been studied almost exclusively in the American grain, and critics have overwhelmingly stressed his relation to Emerson, Thoreau, Dickinson, and other writers of the New England Renaissance. In fact, Frost was more powerfully influenced by English verse, particularly the English pastoral tradition of Wordsworth, Keats, and Hardy, than any other American poet of his time.

Frost adopted many of the principles expressed in Wordsworth's Preface to the *Lyrical Ballads* (1802) concerning the diction, people, places, and social conditions appropriate to poetry. Like Wordsworth, he "chose incidents and situations from common life," described them in "language really used by men," and made these "incidents and situations interesting by tracing in them . . . the primary laws of our nature." He preferred people in "low and rustic life" because they "speak a plainer and more emphatic language," express elemental feelings, and reveal "the essential passions of the heart." The "manners of rural life" are "more easily comprehended and are more durable . . . because in that condition the passions of men are incorporated with the beautiful and permanent forms of nature." In an early interview Frost traced the source of his fundamental theory back to Wordsworth: "Language only really exists in the mouths of men. Wordsworth was right in trying to reproduce in his poetry not only the words—in their limited range, too, actually used in common speech—but their sound."

Frost also believed that "tones, pauses and rushes and intensities of sound are more revealing than the definition value [that is, the specific meaning] of the words," and told his friend John Bartlett, "I alone of English writers have consciously set myself to make music out of what I may call the sound of sense." But this theory, like his bountiful allusions, was firmly rooted in the English literary tradition. In "An Essay on Criticism" (1711), for example, Pope declares, "The sound must seem an echo to the sense," and in chapter 9 of Carroll's *Alice's Adventures in Wonderland* (1865), the Duchess tells Alice, "Take care of the sense, and the sounds will take care of themselves." When advocating the primacy of sound over sense, Frost defined a sentence as "a sound in itself on which other sounds called words may be strung." Then, stretching his case to an unbelievable degree, he insisted that the *tone* of voice is not only vital, but conveys more than the precise meaning: "the sentence sound often says *more* than the words. It may even as in irony convey a meaning opposite to the words. . . . I shall show the sentence sound saying all that the sentence conveys with little or no help from the meaning of the words."

II

A Boy's Will, published in London by David Nutt on about April 1, 1913, was dedicated, like all but one of his books brought out in her lifetime, to Frost's wife, Elinor. It took its title from a favorite boyhood poem, "My Lost Youth," in which Longfellow wrote: "A boy's will is the wind's will, / And the thoughts of youth are long, long thoughts." In Frost, as in Longfellow, the boy tends to brood about the past and has emotions as variable as the wind. The original edition contained vague and not especially illuminating glosses on the poems, after the fashion of Yeats's *The Wind Among the Reeds* (1899). The glosses suggest the considerable difference in age between the thirty-nine-year-old author and the youth in the book, and express the poet's gently ironic attitude toward his rather sentimental and self-pitying hero.

The thirty-two autobiographical poems (three were later dropped, along with all the glosses) reflect the annual cycle of the seasons and move from autumn to autumn, from "My November Guest" to "October." The first poem, "Into My Own," describes Frost's flight in 1894 from Dartmouth College, from Lawrence, Massachusetts, and from his fiancée, Elinor, for a half-serious suicide attempt in the Dismal Swamp of Virginia. After the narrator steals away into the vastness of dark trees, he wonders if those who love him will try to find him:

I do not see why I should e'er turn back,
Or those should not set forth upon my track
To overtake me, who should miss me here
And long to know if still I held them dear.

They would not find me changed from him they knew—
Only more sure of all I thought was true.

As in Poe's "Dream-Land," the narrator of "Into My Own" finds himself (in the positive sense) by running away and becomes surer of what he felt was true—his love for Elinor.

"The Tuft of Flowers," which helped Frost procure a teaching job at Pinkerton Academy, appears toward the end of the cycle and marks his return to society after five years of self-enforced solitude on the farm in Derry. Frost described this book to the editor of the *Youth's Companion,* which had published three of the poems, as "a series of lyrics standing in some such loose relation to each other as a ring of children who have just stopped dancing and let go hands," and called it "The Record of a Phase of Post-adolescence."

A Boy's Will describes the natural elements that Frost would make his permanent poetic property: stars, clouds, leaves, flowers, brooks, birds. Nine of the poems had been published in minor American periodicals between 1906 and 1912, and he retained "My Butterfly" (from the *Independent* of 1894), which stuck out awkwardly amid his more polished work. Frost later recalled that he had written "My Butterfly" by locking himself in the kitchen of his house in Lawrence. While he was composing the poem, his sister Jeanie had tried to batter down the door and break in. In January 1896, unsure of his talent and still trying to find his way, Frost wrote the editor Susan Ward that he feared he was not a poet—or not a very comprehensible one. He later told another friend that in the pure, imagistic description of the second quatrain ("The gray grass is not dappled with the snow") he had struck for the first time his characteristic note. He was sufficiently fond of this poem, inspired by Wordsworth's "To a Butterfly," to include it in *A Boy's Will*. Nevertheless, its archaic diction and sentimental thought (he finds its broken wing amid the withered autumn leaves) made it distinctly inferior to the rest of the book. Frost's tremendous advance as a poet can immediately be seen by comparing "My Butterfly" with "Blue-Butterfly Day" (1921), with its striking imagery and frightening contrast in the razorlike last lines: "They lie closed over in the wind and cling / Where wheels have freshly sliced the April mire."

Frost developed his ideas about the use of everyday language *after* he had written these early poems, which are full of old-fashioned contractions, inversions, and lifeless archaic diction: "I wist . . . Thou didst . . . fain to list . . . fully many a time . . . many and many a year . . . I knew not well myself . . . that frighted thee so oft." Frost's poetic progress from *A Boy's Will* to *North of Boston* becomes clear when one compares "Snatched thee, o'er eager, with ungentle grasp" (the worst line in the former) with the intensely colloquial "What help he is there's no depending on" in "The Death of the Hired Man."

"Ghost House" anticipates the abandoned farms in *North of Boston*. "My November Guest" expresses Frost's sorrowful love for Elinor, in a gray, Hardy-like landscape, as the lovers meet amid "The desolate, deserted trees, / The faded earth, the heavy sky." Hardy's belief, in "Hap" and "Nature's Questioning," that God is either hostile or at best indifferent to the fate of helpless men finds expression in Frost's later dark poems, "The Night Light" and "Bereft." Hardy's use of distant stars to symbolize, in "Wanting Both," the littleness of man amidst the vast cosmos,

> A star looks down on me,
> And says: "Here I and you
> Stand, each in our degree:
> What do you mean to do?"

precisely recurs in Frost's "Stars," where the goddess of wisdom is blind:

> And yet with neither love nor hate,
>   Those stars like some snow-white
> Minerva's snow-white marble eyes
>   Without the gift of sight.

In the ballad "Love and a Question," the bridegroom does not want to allow a woeful stranger into his house to spoil his love on his wedding night. In the powerful "Storm Fear"—thematically related to the later poems "The Fear" and "House Fear"—a blizzard, blowing high snowdrifts, blocks a small family into their house "Till even the comforting barn grows far away" and makes them doubt whether they have the strength to survive the storm. The supplicating "A Prayer in Spring" reflects the change of seasons and portrays a benign God (who becomes malevolent and menacing in greater poems like "Once by the Pacific"). It reveals Frost's intense response to the natural world and, when calling a white orchard "Like nothing else by day, like ghosts by night," contains the finest line in the book.

"The Trial by Existence," "Mowing," and "Reluctance" are the strongest poems. Frost said that the theme, meter, and imagery of Rossetti's "The Blessed Damozel" (1846), which expressed the yearning of the loved one in heaven, inspired "The Trial by Existence." In Frost's poem, dead heroes awake in paradise (the fourth line echoes the Lord's Prayer), amid the fields of asphodel in Hades where Odysseus found Achilles and Patroclus, to discover that they must continue the struggle they had engaged in on earth. Heaven will also be a testing place of man's courage.

"Mowing" continues the pastoral theme that began with Marvell's "The Mower, Against Gardens" and continued with Wordsworth's "The Solitary Reaper," and that Frost himself took up in "The Exposed Nest" and "The Last Mowing":

There was never a sound beside the wood but one,
And that was my long scythe whispering to the ground.
What was it it whispered? I knew not well myself;
Perhaps it was something about the heat of the sun,
Something, perhaps, about the lack of sound—
And that was why it whispered and did not speak.
It was no dream of the gift of idle hours,
Or easy gold at the hand of fay or elf:
Anything more than the truth would have seemed too weak
To the earnest love that laid the swale in rows,
Not without feeble-pointed spikes of flowers
(Pale orchises), and scared a bright green snake.
The fact is the sweetest dream that labor knows.
My long scythe whispered and left the hay to make.

In this poem, Frost said, he came so close to what he longed to achieve that he almost despaired of coming nearer. He was so fond of the second line that he used it again, a few pages later, in "The Tuft of Flowers." The sound of a blade cutting hay can actually sound like the whisper of a human voice, and during the consoling rhythm of repeated motion the mower hears the sound and tries to make out the unspoken sense of what it whispered. Echoing the song from *Cymbeline* ("Fear no more the heat of the sun"), Frost suggests that the truth lies in the physical conditions of summer toil, during which he cut the spiky orchis flowers and scared—but did not harm—the bright green snake. The mower-poet discerns from the whispering scythe, by the end of the morning and the end of the poem, that the thing he *makes*—the hay in the poem and the poem itself—"is the sweetest dream that labor knows."

"The Tuft of Flowers," composed of twenty couplets, describes—like "Mowing"—the pastoral labor of cutting a field of grass and the careful preservation—as in "Rose Pogonias"—of some wildflowers. The narrator of the poem, who follows the absent mower and must turn the cut grass, finds himself alone: "'As all must be,' I said within my heart, / 'Whether they work together or apart.'" A butterfly then leads him to a tall tuft of flowers beside a brook: "A leaping tongue of bloom the scythe had spared / Beside a reedy brook the scythe had bared." The flowers, spared by the mower who rejoiced in their beauty, awaken his senses and enable him to "hear his long scythe whispering to the ground." The flowers also carry a "message," which contradicts the narrator's earlier assumption about the solitude of men and puts him in touch with the kindred spirit of his fellow toiler: "'Men work together,' I told him from the heart, / 'Whether they work together or apart.'"

In "Reluctance," the last poem in the book, Frost returns to the woods and season of the opening poem. After running away, he now comes home and expresses his individualistic credo by asking, in imaginative terms, three rhetorical questions:

> Ah, when to the heart of man
>   Was it ever less than a treason
> To go with the drift of things,
>   To yield with a grace to reason,
> And bow and accept the end
>   Of a love or a season?

Reluctant to accept the norms of conventional behavior, he declares that he will go against the grain, follow his own intuition, and resist what appears to be the end of Elinor's love. The concluding stanza synthesizes the theme of mutability that dominates *A Boy's Will*.

III

ON MAY 15, 1914, David Nutt published—in a green buckram volume at three shillings and sixpence—Frost's second and finest book, *North of Boston*. Frost began writing this work in 1905 and completed "the bulk of it" in 1913. Assuming that English readers would associate Boston with the town in Lincolnshire, the critic T. E. Hulme wanted Frost to change the title to the Virgilian *Yankee Eclogues,* and Ezra Pound called his influential review "Modern Georgics." Other provisional titles were *New England Eclogues,* the more familiar *New England Hill Folk,* and *Farm Servants, and Other People.* The publication of this book greatly enhanced Frost's status among the English poets.

North of Boston signaled Frost's change of emphasis from solitary to social beings. In his dedication to Elinor he called it "This Book of People," and in a note said that "Mending Wall," which considers beliefs that separate men, takes up the theme where "The Tuft of Flowers" laid it down. Despite its social emphasis, most of the characters in *North of Boston* experience great loneliness.

The poems in *A Boy's Will* are short lyrics, those in *North of Boston* are ironic and often witty dramatic dialogues after the fashion of Browning and Kipling. In the second volume Frost moves from archaic diction to colloquial language and combines country lore with metaphysical conceits. As the critic Lawrence Lipking observed: "Voices clash against each other. . . . A harder broken speech replaces the language of flowers. And through that act of reinterpretation"—of defining his new poetic identity—"Frost becomes Frost."

In *North of Boston* Frost stakes out his poetic territory and begins to set his regionalism against the cosmopolitanism of Pound, Eliot, and Stevens. He had no interest in urban or industrial life and, unlike contemporaries from Yeats to Robert Lowell, rarely wrote poems about historical events, living or dead friends, painting, or music. Though he lived for substantial periods in Michigan, Florida, and Texas, and later traveled to France, Cuba, Brazil, Peru, Israel, Greece, and Russia, Frost never wrote about these places. When he described exotic locales—Mexico, the Madeiras, the Vale of Kashmir—he based his poems on the historical accounts of William Prescott, Richard Hakluyt, and Marco Polo. Apart from a few poems about California and England, he was, wherever he lived, an exclusively New England poet.

Frost describes the nineteenth-century New England phenomenon of subsistence farming. The desolation, decay, and desperation; the exhaustion, estrangement, and isolation; the violence, mutilation, terror, madness, and death in *North of Boston* capture the last moments of a dying race. Amy Lowell, the grande dame of Boston, once told Frost that she had left her summer place in New Hampshire because she could not stand the people. When he asked her what was wrong with the people, she told him to read his own books and find out. Yet Frost's poetry, like Hardy's, is strengthened by his intense focus on and intimate knowledge of one region. He values country over city, worldly experience over school learning, personal independence over government interference. His magnificent description of the natural—but often threatening—world expresses his belief in self-reliance and rugged individualism. These qualities had largely vanished from the anonymous life of urban and industrial America, and lost city dwellers still longed for them as part of their Puritan and frontier heritage.

Frost's poems set themes in ironic opposition and unite, as Jackson Bate wrote of Coleridge, "scope and depth, philosophical range and immediacy of detail, psychological insight and emotional suggestiveness." When the poet Randall Jarrell asked Frost about the poems in *North of Boston*—"Home Burial," "A Servant to Servants," "The Housekeeper," "The Fear"—in which an emotionally oppressed woman finally reveals her deepest feelings, Frost said that "the woman loses," but "she loses in a strange way, she pulls the whole thing down with her. She has that satisfaction." Frost understood the suffering and frustration of these hardworking, yet impoverished, women, who took grim pleasure in venting their anger and achieving revenge.

The sixteen subtle poems in *North of Boston* have great technical and thematic interest. "The Death of the Hired Man" includes three very different characters, one of them offstage, who are revealed entirely through dialogue. Silas, the hired man, has instinctively returned to his lair like a wounded animal. The farmer and his wife discuss how to deal with this unwelcome guest, for whom they feel partly responsible. The poem considers how much dignity is due to a useless and derelict old man. "A Hundred Collars" contrasts the countrified, expansive, and witty bill collector, Lafayette, with the urban, repressed, and solemn teacher, Magoon. It is quite funny and contains two striking similes. The tight collars choke Lafe "like a nursery tree / When it outgrows the wire band of its name tag" and his spoiled horse, Jemima, turns in at every house along the road "As if she had some sort of curvature." "The Black Cottage" ends with the same visual power and dramatic intensity characteristic of Hemingway's early stories:

> He struck the clapboards,
> Fierce heads looked out; small bodies pivoted.
> We rose to go. Sunset blazed on the windows.

"A Servant to Servants" contains a hair-raising description of a crazy naked man, locked in a cage, who screams obscenities as the young bride and groom lie in the next room. "The Self-Seeker" is based on a mechanical accident that badly crushed the feet of Frost's friend Carl Burell and crippled him. His casual negotiations with the company lawyer are interrupted by the charming intrusion of a little girl, who brings rare specimens of flowers he can no longer find himself and emphasizes the priceless value of what he has lost. The conclusion of "The Wood-Pile," with its faint echo of Gray's "Elegy" ("They kept the noise*less* tenor of their *way*"), contains the finest lines in the book:

> To warm the frozen swamp as best it could
> With the slow smoke*less* burning of de*cay*.

The best poems in *North of Boston* are "Mending Wall," "Home Burial," and Frost's masterpiece, "After Apple-Picking." "Mending Wall" (like "The Road Not Taken," "Birches," and "Stopping by Woods on a Snowy Evening") has become overly familiar through endless reprintings in school anthologies. Like the frequently reproduced *Sunflowers* of Van Gogh, it has lost a good deal of its freshness and impact. Frost once saw the mindless statement "Good fences make good neighbours" (originally made by his Derry friend, the "old-stone savage" Napoleon Guay), used on an advertisement for a prefabricated picket fence.

Frost himself said the poem concerned "the impossibility of drawing sharp lines and making exact distinctions between good and bad or between almost any two abstractions." But he clearly stands with the narrator who questions the very need to have a wall and repeats his belief: "Something there is that doesn't love a wall." That "something," a natural force, which breaks down the wall and indicates the poet's point of view is—of course—frost. His allusion to Matthew 24:2 clarifies the theme by connecting the inevitable and proper destruction of the wall in the poem to Christ's fierce prophecy about the iniquitous Temple of Herod in Jerusalem: "There shall not be left here one stone upon another, that shall not be thrown down."

"Home Burial" (whose title suggests both burial at home and the burial of home life) describes with startling honesty the effect on Elinor of the death in 1900 of their three-year-old son, Elliott. It speaks of woe that is in marriage. The poem portrays two kinds of grief: the man hides his feelings and wants to resume life; the woman, overcome by her feelings, wants to mourn. He asks to be let into her grief; she shuts him out. Though the woman fails to understand the man, Frost sympathizes with her point of view. In this respect, his dramatic account of an agonizing situation resembles Hemingway's "Hills Like White Elephants" (1927). In that story, a young man, trying to convince his mistress to have an abortion, talks too much (as the woman remains rather silent) and alienates her affection. As Frost explained in his notebook: "His wife listened to his ruthless talk and for a long time half-believed him. Reckless of losing her he still talked on." In Frost's poem, the man perceives: "My words are nearly always an offence."

As the man talks on, the woman becomes fearful, cowering, and withdrawn. Their quarrel on the narrow staircase of their house concerns perception. She calls him a blind creature who cannot see, he claims to see what is bothering her. Her grief is focused on the family graveyard, visible from the house, where their recently dead first infant is buried. (The baby's mound of earth contrasts with the solid stones of the older dead.) When he dares to mention the fresh grave, she cries, "Don't, don't, don't, don't," which echoes through the poem. It has the same effect as the "Never, never, never, never, never" in *King Lear* and the "please please please please please please stop talking" in Hemingway's story. Frost told his friend Sidney Cox that "the four 'don'ts' were the supreme thing in it."

The woman denies him the right to speak of her loss. Stifled by her existence, she threatens to leave as he pleads with her to stay. He claims her grief is excessive ("You overdo it a little"); she maintains that he has no feelings. She then condemns him for the way he—almost joyfully (for he was physically absorbed in the cathartic work)—dug the child's grave:

Making the gravel leap and leap in air,
Leap up, like that, like that, and land so lightly

and for coming into the house "with the stains on your shoes / Of the fresh earth from your own baby's grave." He replies that he is cursed, like Job, both by the death of his child and by his wife's imprecations. But she continues to condemn him by repeating his innocent but apparently callous words: "Three foggy mornings and one rainy day / Will rot the best birch fence a man can build." By saying this, he was thinking of fences—not their implications. But she connects the fence to the child in a horrible way, twists his words to mean that their baby was doomed to rot as surely and as quickly as the fence. Why make a fence, if it rots in only three days, he seems to be saying, and why make a baby, who now *rots* in the ground. She prefers to be alone with her grief ("I won't, I won't!" echoes her previous "don'ts"); he wants to make his "way back to life." When he utterly fails to persuade her by words, he threatens to follow her out of the house and force her back into life.

"After Apple-Picking" has often been compared to Keats's "Ode to Autumn," as if it were primarily a celebration of harvest. But its elevated diction (quite distinct from anything else in the book) as well as its images, mood, and theme, all suggest a greater affinity with Keats's "Ode to a Nightingale." In that weary, drowsy poem the speaker longs to escape through art, symbolized by the nightingale, from the pain of the real world and to melt into the welcome oblivion of death:

> My heart aches, and a drowsy numbness pains
> My sense, as though of hemlock I had drunk,
> Or emptied some dull opiate to the drains
> One minute past, and Lethe-wards had sunk.

Frost's narrator, standing on the earth but looking upward, is also suspended between the real and the dream worlds:

> My long two-pointed ladder's sticking through a tree
> Toward heaven still,
> And there's a barrel that I didn't fill

The long and short lines, the irregular rhyme scheme, the recurrent participles (indicating work), the slow tempo, and the incantatory rhythm all suggest that repetitive labor has drained away his energy. The perfume of the apples—equated through "essence" with profound rest—has the narcotic, almost sensual effect of ether. Frost's speaker, like Keats's, is suffused with drowsy numbness, yet enters the visionary state necessary to artistic creation:

> Essence of winter sleep is on the night,
> The scent of apples: I am drowsing off.
> I cannot rub the strangeness from my sight
> I got from looking through a pane of glass
> I skimmed this morning from the drinking trough

The glassy piece of ice—which distorts, transforms, and makes the familiar seem strange—is, like Keats's nightingale, a symbol of art. In his dream state (the word "sleep" occurs six times in the poem),

> Magnified apples appear and disappear,
> Stem end and blossom end,
> And every fleck of russet showing clear.

and he rhythmically sways on the ladder when the boughs bend with his weight. As the apples are gathered—and the poem written—he becomes both physically and mentally exhausted:

> For I have had too much
> Of apple-picking: I am overtired
> Of the great harvest I myself desired.

He needs to regenerate himself, like the hibernating woodchuck, by a long, deathlike winter sleep, so he will be ready to reenter the poet's dream world and achieve another spurt of creativity. In "After Apple-Picking" Frost achieves a perfect fusion of pastoral and poetic labor.

IV

EAGER TO capitalize on the success of *North of Boston*, in November 1916 Frost's American publisher Henry Holt brought out his next book, *Mountain Interval*, in an edition of four thousand copies. Always rather reluctant to part with his poems, Frost felt that he had been pressed into publishing his third book. He thought it lacked formal unity and "was just a bunch of poems slapped together, not judged and weighed like the previous volumes." He had written part of the book before he went to England and several of the poems—"Birches," "Putting in the Seed," "The Hill Wife," and "The Sound of the Trees"—while living in Gloucestershire. Firmly rooted in the English pastoral tradition, the book includes both rhymed lyrics and dramatic narratives in blank verse, along with a ballad and three poems for children. Frost's characteristic themes of isolation, loneliness, and fear are expressed in "An Old Man's Winter Night," "The Hill Wife," and "Snow," and sudden violence and death occur in "The Vanishing Red" and "'Out, Out—'."

In "Christmas Trees," a holiday poem, a city slicker tries unsuccessfully to swindle a countryman. In "The Exposed Nest," partly inspired by Burns's "To a Mouse" and Clare's "Mouse's Nest," the narrator saves vulnerable young birds whose nest has been exposed by mowing. "The Telephone" describes a fanciful talk, through the medium of flowers, between the speaker and his wife. "Meeting and Passing," like Hardy's "A Man Was Drawing Near Me," recounts a brief but telling moment of recognition.

"The Cow in Apple Time," a charming and witty poem with tragic implications, imitates the dramatic repetitions of John Clare's great poem "Badger." Clare describes the savage and pitiful pursuit of a badger in an urgent series of pronouns and active verbs—"He tries . . . He turns . . . He drives . . . He falls"—and concludes with sudden horror. Frost's poem describes a cow, crazily drunk on fallen apples and "having tasted fruit" (or evil):

She scorns a pasture withering to the root.
She runs from tree to tree where lie and sweeten
The windfalls spiked with stubble and worm-eaten.
She leaves them bitten when she has to fly.
She bellows on a knoll against the sky.
Her udder shrivels and the milk goes dry.

"Hyla Brook," where late the tree frogs sang, opens suddenly with "By June our brook's run out of song and speed." The water has gone underground and the frogs' shouts through the mist now seem "Like ghost of sleigh-bells in a ghost of snow" (which echoes Frost's earlier line, "Like nothing else by day, like ghosts by night"). Though the brook is now nothing more than a precious memory, the speaker asserts his unqualified love for the change of seasons in his native region, whatever its defects:

A brook to none but who remember long.
This as it will be seen is other far
Than with brooks taken otherwhere in song.
We love the things we love for what they are.

"The Oven Bird," about an American warbler with an oven-shaped nest and a harsh song, follows and complements "Hyla Brook." The poem opens with "There is a singer everyone [around here] has heard" and then describes the harsh, midsummer song that reverberates through the wood, when other birds have already stopped singing, and announces the coming of autumn. Echoing Keats's "Ode to a Nightingale," and linking the oven bird's song to the similarly diminished Hyla Brook, Frost emphasizes the need to persist, as powers weaken, in singing—or loving or writing:

The bird would cease and be as other birds
But that he knows in singing not to sing.

The question that he frames in all but words
Is what to make of a diminished thing.

Though *North of Boston* was Frost's greatest book, each subsequent volume contained a few masterpieces. The outstanding poems in *Mountain Interval* are the justly famous "Birches" and "The Road Not Taken" as well as "Putting in the Seed" and "'Out, Out—'." "Birches" connects poetic aspiration and physical love. It begins with a fanciful image ("I like to think") of a boy swinging on and bending birches. It then shifts to a brilliant description of ice-laden branches blown by the wind that "cracks and crazes [suggesting cracked glazes] their enamel." Inspired by medieval cosmology and by a famous passage from Shelley's "Adonais" (an elegy for Keats about poetic power cut off in mid-career by death), Frost writes of all the broken ice-glass: "You'd think the inner dome of heaven had fallen." He then returns to the swinger-of-birches theme as the boy, like the future poet, launches out at the proper time, keeps his poise, and climbs carefully. Swinging himself on the branches *"Toward* heaven," he'd

like to get away from earth awhile
And then come back to it and begin over. . . .
        Earth's the right place for love:
I don't know where it's likely to go better.

Opposing the Platonic view of idealized love, Frost believes that earth, not heaven, is the right place, because love should be physical and tested against the realities of life.

"Putting in the Seed," one of Frost's most sensual poems, is also a celebration of physical love. The man puts the seed in the woman as well as in the ground and, as metaphor merges with reality, the procreative poem works perfectly on both levels. The speaker invites the responsive woman to "become like me, / Slave to a springtime passion for the earth." He capitalizes the life-giving moment, inspired by both passion and love, and the birth of the child follows naturally from the arched bodies in the sexual act. The infant shoulders its way out of the womb and into the world just as a new seed comes alive by pushing through the earth:

> How Love burns through the Putting in the Seed
> On through the watching for that early birth
> When, just as the soil tarnishes with weed,
> The sturdy seedling with arched body comes
> Shouldering its way and shedding the earth crumbs.

Though "'Out, Out—'" is one of his greatest poems, Frost always felt that (like "Home Burial") it was too cruel to read in public. The poem was based on an incident that took place in Bethlehem, New Hampshire, in March 1901. Raymond Fitzgerald, the son of Frost's friend, was cutting wood with a sawing machine when he accidentally hit the loose pulley and badly cut and lacerated his hand. Raymond was taken into the house and a doctor was called, but he died of shock.

The title refers to the blood gushing out of the mutilated body as well as to Macbeth's speech on the death of his queen. Shakespeare's tragic hero emphasizes the brevity and meaninglessness of human existence:

> Out, out, brief candle!
> Life's but a walking shadow, a poor player
> That struts and frets his hour upon the stage
> And then is heard no more. It is a tale
> Told by an idiot, full of sound and fury,
> Signifying nothing.
> (5. 5. 23)

Frost's poem opens suddenly with the dangerous, menacing machine producing sweet-scented sawdust in a tranquil mountain setting. The first line is repeated more emphatically in the seventh, as the setting sun that marks the end of the day's work foreshadows the extinction of the brief candle of life. Just at that moment the saw seems to take on a life of its own by leaping "out at the boy's hand" and causing a pathetic wound:

> The boy's first outcry was a rueful laugh,
> As he swung toward them holding up the hand
> Half in appeal, but half as if to keep
> The life from spilling.

The boy begs them not to cut his hand off, but the hand is already gone. The ending, as life leaks out in a series of short phrases, is truly terrifying:

> The doctor put him in the dark of ether.
> He lay and puffed his lips out with his breath.
> And then—the watcher at his pulse took fright.
> No one believed. They listened at his heart.
> Little—less—nothing!—and that ended it.
> No more to build on there. And they, since they
> Were not the one dead, turned to their affairs.

The conclusion of this poem, which echoes the magnificent last line of "The Fear"—"It touched, it struck, it clattered and went out"—is a bitter comment on the callous indifference to human suffering. It inspired (along with Brueghel's painting *The Fall of Icarus*) the ending of Auden's "Musée des Beaux Arts" (1940):

> and the expensive delicate ship that must have seen
> Something amazing, a boy falling out of the sky,
> Had somewhere to get to and sailed calmly on.

"The Road Not Taken" is a mildly satiric comment on the self-tormenting ambivalence of the English poet Edward Thomas, Frost's closest friend. But it has deeper roots in an uncanny experience that Frost described in a letter to Susan Ward on February 10, 1912, six months before leaving for England. While walking on "two lonely cross-roads," neither "much travelled," after a winter storm, Frost met a silent, approaching, Poe-like figure who seemed to be his spectral double—"like myself . . . my own image . . . this other self":

Judge then how surprised I was the other evening as I came down one to see a man, who to my own unfamiliar eyes and in the dusk looked for all the world like myself, coming down the other, his approach to the point where our paths must intersect being so timed that unless one of us pulled up we must inevitably collide. I felt as if I was going to meet my own image in a slanting mirror. Or may I say I felt as we slowly converged on the same point with the same noiseless yet laborious strides as if we were two images about to float together with the uncrossing of someone's eyes. I verily expected to take up or absorb this other self and feel the stronger by the addition for the three-mile journey home. But I didn't go forward to the touch. I stood in wonderment and let him pass by.

The words "lonely cross-roads," "converged," and "much travelled" in the letter become "Two roads diverged" and "less traveled by" at the beginning and end of the poem, and the inevitability of "converged" turns into the perplexity of "diverged." The two figures in the letter (Frost and his *Doppelgänger*) merge with Frost and Thomas (since Frost was deeply involved in all Thomas's conflicts about his marriage and service in the war) to produce in the poem the impossible desire to "travel both [roads] / And be one traveler." Though the poet takes the other road because it wanted wear and has the better claim, he also realizes that both roads are really about the same. The most important thing, therefore, is not the road itself, but the *decision* about which road to take:

I shall be telling this with a sigh
Somewhere ages and ages hence:
Two roads diverged in a wood, and I—
I took the one less traveled by,
And that has made all the difference.

The first two lines in this final stanza are weak—the "sigh" is unequal to the emotion expressed, the near-cliché "ages and ages" is surrounded by two vague adverbs. The statement that one road is "less traveled by" contradicts "just as fair," "about the same," and "both . . . equally lay." Yet Frost manages to convey the feeling of a momentous and life-changing resolution by repeating the opening line ("Two roads diverged in a yellow wood") and by the clinching word "difference." He also draws on the associative power of the last lines of Wordsworth's great lyric "She dwelt among the untrodden ways" to emphasize, in a single word, the crucial opposition to all the sameness in the poem:

She lived unknown, and few could know
    When Lucy ceased to be;
But she is in her grave, and, oh,
    The difference to me!

The concluding sentence of William James's "The Will to Believe" (a quotation from Virginia Woolf's uncle, Fitzjames Stephen), which Frost had read at Harvard and taught in school, suggests the philosophic difficulty of such momentous decisions and the positive, stoical attitude one has to adopt in order to survive: "If we take the wrong road we shall be dashed to pieces. We do not certainly know whether there is any right one. What must we do? . . . Act for the best, hope for the best, and take what comes." In May 1915, three months before it appeared in the *Atlantic Monthly,* Frost revealed in a letter that the ambivalence in the poem was his own as well as Edward Thomas's and asserted that he had always been right to choose the less practical and more poetical way. Like Thomas, Frost had to deal with the momentous question of what to do with his precious talent: "I have been pulled two ways and torn in two all my life. But by the Lord Harry every time I have taken the way it almost seemed as if I ought not to take, I have been justified somehow by the result. It scares me to say it. . . . I don't say I have done well for my family—I have done badly, but I've always made some little gain for them when I took a [chance]."

v

OFTEN ASKED about poetic inspiration—how a poem actually comes into being—Frost carefully formulated his ideas on this crucial subject. He felt that transformations in his life—traveling around, changing jobs, moving houses, even a high fever—stimulated his writing. He emphasized the lively play of mind and play of words, and said: "You've got to snap the quip to make Pegasus prance." He wrote an essay in praise of extravagance and, like Thoreau, feared "only lest my expression may not be extravagant enough." The best way to get started, Frost told a correspondent, was with one original metaphor: "Write down your luckiest comparison simply and unaffectedly enough and you can hardly help having poetry. That's the whole game. . . . Make one good distinct figure of speech that's all your own and you are started on the road to poetry."

Frost believed that a poem should be written in a single, free-flowing run. He compared composing verse to sliding down a hill on a sled and declared: "I never wrote anything without thinking: 'This is it!'" Like Plato's symbolic horses, whose creative energy had to be harnessed by a charioteer in order to be transformed into art, Frost wrote, in a punning passage, that the first rush of inspiration must be tempered by wordplay in order to avoid the twin dangers of cliché and aestheticism: "Emotional plunge comes first of course, but it simply must be harnessed to the wit mill to turn mots, phrases, stanzas and notions. Wit gives a poet something else to play with than the conventional old poetic resentments against machinery, money and the humdrum of instituted society. It protects the professor of beauty from becoming a kalomaniac [someone crazy about beauty]. I may make too much of nimbleness. But even at my most serious give me nimbleness and 'spree.'"

A brilliant teacher from youth to old age, Frost had many valuable—and always pragmatic—ideas about the imaginative act, the rush of inspiration, the methods of revision, and the pressures of publication. He was not a tormented, self-destructive poet, but one who loved the play of the imagination, took joy in his creation, and believed that "poetry spoils you for anything else in life." Fond of social life and a great talker, in middle and old age he loved to draw large crowds at lectures around the country. But he also needed and valued solitude and reflection. Reflecting on the apparent laziness of his early years, he declared that loafing had a great deal to do with being creative, and that for proper artistic growth there must be idleness, which had been the making of him. Ever confident of his creative powers and his longevity, he told a friend: "The clearest hint I have of immortality is that I have time to burn. I've always known somehow that I've had time to burn." These early books are the culmination of Frost's long, solitary, and formative years, when he took all the time he needed to become a poet.

The text of these poems is based on the first editions: *A Boy's Will* (London: David Nutt, 1913), *North of Boston* (London: David Nutt, 1914), and *Mountain Interval* (New York: Henry Holt, 1916).

—*Jeffrey Meyers*

A BOY'S WILL

TO E.M.F

INTO MY OWN

One of my wishes is that those dark trees,
So old and firm they scarcely show the breeze,
Were not, as 'twere, the merest mask of gloom,
But stretched away unto the edge of doom.[1]

I should not be withheld but that some day
Into their vastness I should steal away,
Fearless of ever finding open land,
Or highway where the slow wheel pours the sand.

I do not see why I should e'er turn back,
Or those should not set forth upon my track
To overtake me, who should miss me here
And long to know if still I held them dear.

They would not find me changed from him they knew—
Only more sure of all I thought was true.

GHOST HOUSE

I dwell in a lonely house I know
That vanished many a summer ago,
    And left no trace but the cellar walls,
    And a cellar in which the daylight falls,
And the purple-stemmed wild raspberries grow.

O'er ruined fences the grape-vines shield
The woods come back to the mowing field;
    The orchard tree has grown one copse
    Of new wood and old where the woodpecker chops;
The footpath down to the well is healed.

I dwell with a strangely aching heart
In that vanished abode there far apart
    On that disused and forgotten road
    That has no dust-bath now for the toad.
Night comes; the black bats tumble and dart;

The whippoorwill is coming to shout
And hush and cluck and flutter about:
    I hear him begin far enough away
    Full many a time to say his say
Before he arrives to say it out.

It is under the small, dim, summer star,
I know not who these mute folk are
    Who share the unlit place with me—
    Those stones out under the low-limbed tree
Doubtless bear names that the mosses mar.

They are tireless folk, but slow and sad,
Though two, close-keeping, are lass and lad,—
   With none among them that ever sings,
   And yet, in view of how many things,
As sweet companions as might be had.

MY NOVEMBER GUEST

My Sorrow, when she's here with me,
　　Thinks these dark days of autumn rain
Are beautiful as days can be;
She loves the bare, the withered tree;
　　She walks the sodden pasture lane.

Her pleasure will not let me stay.
　　She talks and I am fain to list:[2]
She's glad the birds are gone away,
She's glad her simple worsted gray
　　Is silver now with clinging mist.

The desolate, deserted trees,
　　The faded earth, the heavy sky,
The beauties she so truly sees,
She thinks I have no eye for these,
　　And vexes me for reason why.

Not yesterday I learned to know
　　The love of bare November days
Before the coming of the snow,
But it were vain to tell her so,
　　And they are better for her praise.

LOVE AND A QUESTION

A stranger came to the door at eve,
    And he spoke the bridegroom fair.
He bore a green-white stick in his hand,
    And, for all burden, care.
He asked with the eyes more than the lips
    For a shelter for the night,
And he turned and looked at the road afar
    Without a window light.

The bridegroom came forth into the porch
    With "Let us look at the sky,
And question what of the night to be,
    Stranger, you and I."
The woodbine leaves littered the yard,
    The woodbine berries were blue,
Autumn, yes, winter was in the wind;
    "Stranger, I wish I knew."

Within, the bride in the dusk alone
    Bent over the open fire,
Her face rose-red with the glowing coal
    And the thought of the heart's desire.
The bridegroom looked at the weary road,
    Yet saw but her within,
And wished her heart in a case of gold[3]
    And pinned with a silver pin.

The bridegroom thought it little to give
   A dole of bread, a purse,
A heartfelt prayer for the poor of God,
   Or for the rich a curse;
But whether or not a man was asked
   To mar the love of two
By harboring woe in the bridal house,
   The bridegroom wished he knew.

A LATE WALK

When I go up through the mowing field,
   The headless aftermath,
Smooth-laid like thatch with the heavy dew,
   Half closes the garden path.

And when I come to the garden ground,
   The whir of sober birds
Up from the tangle of withered weeds
   Is sadder than any words.

A tree beside the wall stands bare,
   But a leaf that lingered brown,
Disturbed, I doubt not, by my thought,
   Comes softly rattling down.

I end not far from my going forth
   By picking the faded blue
Of the last remaining aster flower
   To carry again to you.

STARS

How countlessly they congregate
    O'er our tumultuous snow,
Which flows in shapes as tall as trees
    When wintry winds do blow!—

As if with keenness for our fate,
    Our faltering few steps on
To white rest, and a place of rest
    Invisible at dawn—

And yet with neither love nor hate,
    Those stars like some snow-white
Minerva's snow-white marble eyes
    Without the gift of sight.

STORM FEAR

When the wind works against us in the dark,
And pelts with snow
The lower chamber window on the east,
And whispers with a sort of stifled bark,
The beast,
"Come out! Come out!"—
It costs no inward struggle not to go,
Ah, no!
I count our strength,
Two and a child,
Those of us not asleep subdued to mark
How the cold creeps as the fire dies at length,—
How drifts are piled,
Dooryard and road ungraded,
Till even the comforting barn grows far away
And my heart owns a doubt
Whether 'tis in us to arise with day
And save ourselves unaided.

WIND AND WINDOW FLOWER

Lovers, forget your love,
    And list to the love of these,
She a window flower,
    And he a winter breeze.

When the frosty window veil
    Was melted down at noon,
And the cagèd yellow bird
    Hung over her in tune,

He marked her through the pane,
    He could not help but mark,
And only passed her by,
    To come again at dark.

He was a winter wind,
    Concerned with ice and snow,
Dead weeds and unmated birds,
    And little of love could know.

But he sighed upon the sill,
    He gave the sash a shake,
As witness all within
    Who lay that night awake.

Perchance he half prevailed
    To win her for the flight
From the firelit looking-glass
    And warm stove-window light.

But the flower leaned aside
    And thought of naught to say,
And morning found the breeze
    A hundred miles away.

TO THE THAWING WIND

Come with rain, O loud Southwester!
Bring the singer, bring the nester;
Give the buried flower a dream;
Make the settled snow-bank steam;
Find the brown beneath the white;
But whate'er you do to-night,
Bathe my window, make it flow,
Melt it as the ices go;
Melt the glass and leave the sticks
Like a hermit's crucifix;
Burst into my narrow stall;
Swing the picture on the wall;
Run the rattling pages o'er;
Scatter poems on the floor;
Turn the poet out of door.

A PRAYER IN SPRING

Oh, give us pleasure in the flowers to-day;
And give us not to think so far away
As the uncertain harvest; keep us here
All simply in the springing of the year.

Oh, give us pleasure in the orchard white,
Like nothing else by day, like ghosts by night;
And make us happy in the happy bees,[4]
The swarm dilating round the perfect trees.

And make us happy in the darting bird
That suddenly above the bees is heard,
The meteor that thrusts in with needle bill,
And off a blossom in mid air stands still.

For this is love and nothing else is love,
The which it is reserved for God above
To sanctify to what far ends He will,
But which it only needs that we fulfil.

FLOWER-GATHERING

I left you in the morning,
And in the morning glow,
You walked a way beside me
To make me sad to go.
Do you know me in the gloaming,
Gaunt and dusty gray with roaming?
Are you dumb because you know me not,
Or dumb because you know?

All for me? And not a question
For the faded flowers gay
That could take me from beside you
For the ages of a day?
They are yours, and be the measure
Of their worth for you to treasure,
The measure of the little while
That I've been long away.

ROSE POGONIAS[5]

A saturated meadow,
   Sun-shaped and jewel-small,
A circle scarcely wider
   Than the trees around were tall;
Where winds were quite excluded,
   And the air was stifling sweet
With the breath of many flowers,—
   A temple of the heat.

There we bowed us in the burning,
   As the sun's right worship is,
To pick where none could miss them
   A thousand orchises;[6]
For though the grass was scattered,
   Yet every second spear
Seemed tipped with wings of color,
   That tinged the atmosphere.

We raised a simple prayer
   Before we left the spot,
That in the general mowing
   That place might be forgot;
Or if not all so favoured,
   Obtain such grace of hours,
That none should mow the grass there
   While so confused with flowers.

ASKING FOR ROSES

A house that lacks, seemingly, mistress and master,
   With doors that none but the wind ever closes,
Its floor all littered with glass and with plaster;
   It stands in a garden of old-fashioned roses.

I pass by that way in the gloaming with Mary;
   "I wonder," I say, "who the owner of those is."
"Oh, no one you know," she answers me airy,
   "But one we must ask if we want any roses."

So we must join hands in the dew coming coldly
   There in the hush of the wood that reposes,
And turn and go up to the open door boldly,
   And knock to the echoes as beggars for roses.

"Pray, are you within there, Mistress Who-were-you?"
   'Tis Mary that speaks and our errand discloses.
"Pray, are you within there? Bestir you, bestir you!
   'Tis summer again; there's two come for roses.

"A word with you, that of the singer recalling—
   Old Herrick: a saying that every maid knows is
A flower unplucked is but left to the falling,
   And nothing is gained by not gathering roses."

We do not loosen our hands' intertwining
   (Not caring so very much what she supposes),
There when she comes on us mistily shining
   And grants us by silence the boon of her roses.

WAITING

What things for dream there are when spectre-like,[7]
Moving among tall haycocks lightly piled,
I enter alone upon the stubble field,
From which the laborers' voices late have died,
And in the antiphony of afterglow
And rising full moon, sit me down
Upon the full moon's side of the first haycock
And lose myself amid so many alike.

I dream upon the opposing lights of the hour,
Preventing shadow until the moon prevail;
I dream upon the night-hawks peopling heaven,
Each circling each with vague unearthly cry,
Or plunging headlong with fierce twang afar;
And on the bat's mute antics, who would seem
Dimly to have made out my secret place,
Only to lose it when he pirouettes,
And seek it endlessly with purblind haste;
On the last swallow's sweep; and on the rasp
In the abyss of odor and rustle at my back,
That, silenced by my advent, finds once more,
After an interval, his instrument,
And tries once—twice—and thrice if I be there;
And on the worn book of old-golden song[8]
I brought not here to read, it seems, but hold
And freshen in this air of withering sweetness;
But on the memory of one absent most,
For whom these lines when they shall greet her eye.[9]

IN A VALE

When I was young, we dwelt in a vale
   By a misty fen that rang all night,
And thus it was the maidens pale
I knew so well, whose garments trail
   Across the reeds to a window light.

The fen had every kind of bloom,
   And for every kind there was a face,
And a voice that has sounded in my room
Across the sill from the outer gloom.
   Each came singly unto her place,

But all came every night with the mist;
   And often they brought so much to say
Of things of moment to which, they wist,
One so lonely was fain to list,[10]
   That the stars were almost faded away

Before the last went, heavy with dew,
   Back to the place from which she came—
Where the bird was before it flew,
Where the flower was before it grew,
   Where bird and flower were one and the same.

And thus it is I know so well
   Why the flower has odor, the bird has song.
You have only to ask me, and I can tell.
No, not vainly there did I dwell,
   Nor vainly listen all the night long.

A DREAM PANG

I had withdrawn in forest, and my song
Was swallowed up in leaves that blew alway;
And to the forest edge you came one day
(This was my dream) and looked and pondered long,
But did not enter, though the wish was strong:
You shook your pensive head as who should say,
"I dare not—too far in his footsteps stray—
He must seek me would he undo the wrong."

Not far, but near, I stood and saw it all
Behind low boughs the trees let down outside;
And the sweet pang it cost me not to call
And tell you that I saw does still abide.
But 'tis not true that thus I dwelt aloof,
For the wood wakes, and you are here for proof.

IN NEGLECT

They leave us so to the way we took,
    As two in whom they were proved mistaken,
That we sit sometimes in the wayside nook,
With mischievous, vagrant, seraphic look,
    And *try* if we cannot feel forsaken.

THE VANTAGE POINT

If tired of trees I seek again mankind,
   Well I know where to hie me—in the dawn,
   To a slope where the cattle keep the lawn.
There amid lolling juniper reclined,
Myself unseen, I see in white defined
   Far off the homes of men, and farther still,
   The graves of men on an opposing hill,
Living or dead, whichever are to mind.

And if by noon I have too much of these,
   I have but to turn on my arm, and lo,
   The sun-burned hillside sets my face aglow,
My breathing shakes the bluet like a breeze,
   I smell the earth, I smell the bruisèd plant,
   I look into the crater of the ant.

MOWING

There was never a sound beside the wood but one,
And that was my long scythe whispering to the ground.
What was it it whispered? I knew not well myself;
Perhaps it was something about the heat of the sun,
Something, perhaps, about the lack of sound—
And that was why it whispered and did not speak.
It was no dream of the gift of idle hours,
Or easy gold at the hand of fay or elf:
Anything more than the truth would have seemed too weak
To the earnest love that laid the swale in rows,[II]
Not without feeble-pointed spikes of flowers
(Pale orchises), and scared a bright green snake.
The fact is the sweetest dream that labor knows.
My long scythe whispered and left the hay to make.

GOING FOR WATER

The well was dry beside the door,
  And so we went with pail and can
Across the fields behind the house
  To seek the brook if still it ran;

Not loth to have excuse to go,
  Because the autumn eve was fair
(Though chill), because the fields were ours,
  And by the brook our woods were there.

We ran as if to meet the moon
  That slowly dawned behind the trees,
The barren boughs without the leaves,
  Without the birds, without the breeze.

But once within the wood, we paused
  Like gnomes that hid us from the moon,
Ready to run to hiding new
  With laughter when she found us soon.

Each laid on other a staying hand
  To listen ere we dared to look,
And in the hush we joined to make
  We heard, we knew we heard the brook.

A note as from a single place,
  A slender tinkling fall that made
Now drops that floated on the pool
  Like pearls, and now a silver blade.

REVELATION

We make ourselves a place apart
  Behind light words that tease and flout,
But oh, the agitated heart
  Till someone find us really out.

'Tis pity if the case require
  (Or so we say) that in the end
We speak the literal to inspire
  The understanding of a friend.

But so with all, from babes that play
  At hide-and-seek to God afar,
So all who hide too well away
  Must speak and tell us where they are.

THE TRIAL BY EXISTENCE

Even the bravest that are slain
   Shall not dissemble their surprise
On waking to find valor reign,
   Even as on earth, in paradise;
And where they sought without the sword
   Wide fields of asphodel fore'er,
To find that the utmost reward
   Of daring should be still to dare.

The light of heaven falls whole and white
   And is not shattered into dyes,
The light for ever is morning light;
   The hills are verdured pasture-wise;
The angel hosts with freshness go,
   And seek with laughter what to brave;—
And binding all is the hushed snow
   Of the far-distant breaking wave.

And from a cliff-top is proclaimed
   The gathering of the souls for birth,
The trial by existence named,
   The obscuration upon earth.
And the slant spirits trooping by
   In streams and cross- and counter-streams
Can but give ear to that sweet cry
   For its suggestion of what dreams!

And the more loitering are turned
   To view once more the sacrifice

Of those who for some good discerned
  Will gladly give up paradise.
And a white shimmering concourse rolls
  Toward the throne to witness there
The speeding of devoted souls
  Which God makes his especial care.

And none are taken but who will,
  Having first heard the life read out
That opens earthward, good and ill,
  Beyond the shadow of a doubt;
And very beautifully God limns,
  And tenderly, life's little dream,
But naught extenuates or dims,
  Setting the thing that is supreme.

Nor is there wanting in the press
  Some spirit to stand simply forth,
Heroic in its nakedness,
  Against the uttermost of earth.
The tale of earth's unhonored things
  Sounds nobler there than 'neath the sun;
And the mind whirls and the heart sings,
  And a shout greets the daring one.

But always God speaks at the end:
  "One thought in agony of strife
The bravest would have by for friend,
  The memory that he chose the life;
But the pure fate to which you go
  Admits no memory of choice,
Or the woe were not earthly woe
  To which you give the assenting voice."

And so the choice must be again,
   But the last choice is still the same;
And the awe passes wonder then,
   And a hush falls for all acclaim.
And God has taken a flower of gold
   And broken it, and used therefrom
The mystic link to bind and hold
   Spirit to matter till death come.

'Tis of the essence of life here,
   Though we choose greatly, still to lack
The lasting memory at all clear,
   That life has for us on the wrack
Nothing but what we somehow chose;
   Thus are we wholly stripped of pride
In the pain that has but one close,
   Bearing it crushed and mystified.

IN EQUAL SACRIFICE

Thus of old the Douglas did:
He left his land as he was bid
With the royal heart of Robert the Bruce
In a golden case with a golden lid,

To carry the same to the Holy Land;
By which we see and understand
That that was the place to carry a heart
At loyalty and love's command,

And that was the case to carry it in.
The Douglas had not far to win
Before he came to the land of Spain,
Where long a holy war had been

Against the too-victorious Moor;
And there his courage could not endure
Not to strike a blow for God
Before he made his errand sure.

And ever it was intended so,
That a man for God should strike a blow,
No matter the heart he has in charge
For the Holy Land where hearts should go.

But when in battle the foe were met,
The Douglas found him sore beset,
With only strength of the fighting arm
For one more battle passage yet—

And that as vain to save the day
As bring his body safe away—
Only a signal deed to do
And a last sounding word to say.

The heart he wore in a golden chain
He swung and flung forth into the plain,
And followed it crying "Heart or death!"
And fighting over it perished fain.

So may another do of right,
Give a heart to the hopeless fight,
The more of right the more he loves;
So may another redouble might

For a few swift gleams of the angry brand,
Scorning greatly not to demand
In equal sacrifice with his
The heart he bore to the Holy Land.

THE TUFT OF FLOWERS

I went to turn the grass once after one
Who mowed it in the dew before the sun.

The dew was gone that made his blade so keen
Before I came to view the leveled scene.

I looked for him behind an isle of trees;
I listened for his whetstone on the breeze.

But he had gone his way, the grass all mown,
And I must be, as he had been,—alone,

"As all must be," I said within my heart,
"Whether they work together or apart."

But as I said it, swift there passed me by
On noiseless wing a 'wildered butterfly,

Seeking with memories grown dim o'er night
Some resting flower of yesterday's delight.

And once I marked his flight go round and round,
As where some flower lay withering on the ground.

And then he flew as far as eye could see,
And then on tremulous wing came back to me.

I thought of questions that have no reply,
And would have turned to toss the grass to dry;

But he turned first, and led my eye to look
At a tall tuft of flowers beside a brook,

A leaping tongue of bloom the scythe had spared
Beside a reedy brook the scythe had bared.

I left my place to know them by their name,
Finding them butterfly weed when I came.

The mower in the dew had loved them thus,
By leaving them to flourish, not for us,

Nor yet to draw one thought of ours to him.
But from sheer morning gladness at the brim.[12]

The butterfly and I had lit upon,
Nevertheless, a message from the dawn,

That made me hear the wakening birds around,
And hear his long scythe whispering to the ground,

And feel a spirit kindred to my own;
So that henceforth I worked no more alone;

But glad with him, I worked as with his aid,
And weary, sought at noon with him the shade;

And dreaming, as it were, held brotherly speech
With one whose thought I had not hoped to reach.

"Men work together," I told him from the heart,
"Whether they work together or apart."

SPOILS OF THE DEAD

Two fairies it was
   On a still summer day
Came forth in the woods
   With the flowers to play.

The flowers they plucked
   They cast on the ground
For others, and those
   For still others they found.

Flower-guided it was
   That they came as they ran
On something that lay
   In the shape of a man.

The snow must have made
   The feathery bed
When this one fell
   On the sleep of the dead.

But the snow was gone
   A long time ago,
And the body he wore
   Nigh gone with the snow.

The fairies drew near
   And keenly espied
A ring on his hand
   And a chain at his side.

They knelt in the leaves
    And eerily played
With the glittering things,
    And were not afraid.

And when they went home
    To hide in their burrow,
They took them along
    To play with to-morrow.

When *you* came on death,
    Did you not come flower-guided
Like the elves in the wood?
    I remember that I did.

But I recognised death
    With sorrow and dread,
And I hated and hate
    The spoils of the dead.

PAN WITH US

Pan came out of the woods one day,—
His skin and his hair and his eyes were gray,
The gray of the moss of walls were they,—
   And stood in the sun and looked his fill
   At wooded valley and wooded hill.

He stood in the zephyr, pipes in hand,
On a height of naked pasture land;
In all the country he did command
   He saw no smoke and he saw no roof.
   That was well! and he stamped a hoof.

His heart knew peace, for none came here
To this lean feeding save once a year
Someone to salt the half-wild steer,
   Or homespun children with clicking pails
   Who see so little they tell no tales.

He tossed his pipes, too hard to teach
A new-world song, far out of reach,
For a sylvan sign that the blue jay's screech
   And the whimper of hawks beside the sun
   Were music enough for him, for one.

Times were changed from what they were:
Such pipes kept less of power to stir
The fruited bough of the juniper
   And the fragile bluets clustered there
   Than the merest aimless breath of air.

They were pipes of pagan mirth,
And the world had found new terms of worth.
He laid him down on the sun-burned earth
 And ravelled a flower and looked away—
 Play? Play?—What should he play?

THE DEMIURGE'S LAUGH[13]

It was far in the sameness of the wood;
   I was running with joy on the Demon's trail,
Though I knew what I hunted was no true god.
   It was just as the light was beginning to fail
That I suddenly heard—all I needed to hear:
It has lasted me many and many a year.

The sound was behind me instead of before,
   A sleepy sound, but mocking half,
As of one who utterly couldn't care.
   The Demon arose from his wallow to laugh,
Brushing the dirt from his eye as he went;
And well I knew what the Demon meant.

I shall not forget how his laugh rang out.
   I felt as a fool to have been so caught,
And checked my steps to make pretence
   It was something among the leaves I sought
(Though doubtful whether he stayed to see).
Thereafter I sat me against a tree.

NOW CLOSE THE WINDOWS

Now close the windows and hush all the fields;
    If the trees must, let them silently toss;
No bird is singing now, and if there is,
    Be it my loss.

It will be long ere the marshes resume,
    It will be long ere the earliest bird:
So close the windows and not hear the wind,
    But see all wind-stirred.

A LINE-STORM SONG

The line-storm clouds fly tattered and swift,
   The road is forlorn all day,
Where a myriad snowy quartz stones lift,
   And the hoof-prints vanish away.
The roadside flowers, too wet for the bee,
   Expend their bloom in vain.
Come over the hills and far with me,[14]
   And be my love in the rain.

The birds have less to say for themselves
   In the wood-world's torn despair
Than now these numberless years the elves,
   Although they are no less there:
All song of the woods is crushed like some
   Wild, easily shattered rose.
Come, be my love in the wet woods; come,[15]
   Where the boughs rain when it blows.

There is the gale to urge behind
   And bruit our singing down,
And the shallow waters aflutter with wind
   From which to gather your gown.
What matter if we go clear to the west,
   And come not through dry-shod?
For wilding brooch shall wet your breast
   The rain-fresh goldenrod.

Oh, never this whelming east wind swells
    But it seems like the sea's return
To the ancient lands where it left the shells
    Before the age of the fern;
And it seems like the time when after doubt
    Our love came back amain.
Oh, come forth into the storm and rout
    And be my love in the rain.

OCTOBER

O hushed October morning mild,
Thy leaves have ripened to the fall;
To-morrow's wind, if it be wild,
Should waste them all.
The crows above the forest call;
To-morrow they may form and go.
O hushed October morning mild,
Begin the hours of this day slow,
Make the day seem to us less brief.
Hearts not averse to being beguiled,
Beguile us in the way you know;
Release one leaf at break of day;
At noon release another leaf;
One from our trees, one far away;
Retard the sun with gentle mist;[16]
Enchant the land with amethyst.
Slow, slow!
For the grapes' sake, if they were all,
Whose leaves already are burnt with frost,
Whose clustered fruit must else be lost—
For the grapes' sake along the wall.

MY BUTTERFLY

Thine emulous fond flowers are dead, too,[17]
And the daft sun-assaulter, he
That frighted thee so oft, is fled or dead:
Save only me
(Nor is it sad to thee!)
Save only me
There is none left to mourn thee in the fields.

The gray grass is not dappled with the snow;
Its two banks have not shut upon the river;
But it is long ago—
It seems forever—
Since first I saw thee glance,
With all the dazzling other ones,
In airy dalliance,
Precipitate in love,
Tossed, tangled, whirled and whirled above,
Like a limp rose-wreath in a fairy dance.

When that was, the soft mist
Of my regret hung not on all the land,
And I was glad for thee,
And glad for me, I wist.[18]

Thou didst not know, who tottered, wandering on high,
That fate had made thee for the pleasure of the wind,
With those great careless wings,
Nor yet did I.

And there were other things:
It seemed God let thee flutter from his gentle clasp:
Then fearful he had let thee win
Too far beyond him to be gathered in,
Snatched thee, o'ereager, with ungentle grasp.

Ah! I remember me
How once conspiracy was rife
Against my life—
The languor of it and the dreaming fond;
Surging, the grasses dizzied me of thought,
The breeze three odors brought,
And a gem-flower waved in a wand!

Then when I was distraught
And could not speak,
Sidelong, full on my cheek,
What should that reckless zephyr fling
But the wild touch of thy dye-dusty wing!

I found that wing broken to-day!
For thou art dead, I said,
And the strange birds say.
I found it with the withered leaves
Under the eaves.

RELUCTANCE

Out through the fields and the woods
   And over the walls I have wended;
I have climbed the hills of view
   And looked at the world, and descended;
I have come by the highway home,
   And lo, it is ended.

The leaves are all dead on the ground,
   Save those that the oak is keeping
To ravel them one by one
   And let them go scraping and creeping
Out over the crusted snow,
   When others are sleeping.

And the dead leaves lie huddled and still,
   No longer blown hither and thither;
The last lone aster is gone;
   The flowers of the witch-hazel wither;
The heart is still aching to seek,
   But the feet question "Whither?"

Ah, when to the heart of man
   Was it ever less than a treason
To go with the drift of things,
   To yield with a grace to reason,
And bow and accept the end
   Of a love or a season?

NORTH OF BOSTON

TO E.M.F.

THIS BOOK OF PEOPLE

THE PASTURE

I'm going out to clean the pasture spring;
I'll only stop to rake the leaves away
(And wait to watch the water clear, I may):
I shan't be gone long. — You come too.

I'm going out to fetch the little calf
That's standing by the mother. It's so young,
It totters when she licks it with her tongue.
I shan't be gone long. — You come too.

"Mending Wall" takes up the theme where
"The Tuft of Flowers" in
A Boy's Will
laid it down.

MENDING WALL

Something there is that doesn't love a wall,
That sends the frozen-ground-swell under it,
And spills the upper boulders in the sun;
And makes gaps even two can pass abreast.
The work of hunters is another thing:
I have come after them and made repair
Where they have left not one stone on a stone,
But they would have the rabbit out of hiding,
To please the yelping dogs. The gaps I mean,
No one has seen them made or heard them made,
But at spring mending-time we find them there.
I let my neighbour know beyond the hill;
And on a day we meet to walk the line
And set the wall between us once again.
We keep the wall between us as we go.
To each the boulders that have fallen to each.
And some are loaves and some so nearly balls
We have to use a spell to make them balance:
"Stay where you are until our backs are turned!"
We wear our fingers rough with handling them.
Oh, just another kind of out-door game,
One on a side. It comes to little more:
There where it is we do not need the wall:
He is all pine and I am apple orchard.
My apple trees will never get across
And eat the cones under his pines, I tell him.
He only says, "Good fences make good neighbours."
Spring is the mischief in me, and I wonder
If I could put a notion in his head:

"*Why* do they make good neighbours? Isn't it
Where there are cows? But here there are no cows.
Before I built a wall I'd ask to know
What I was walling in or walling out,
And to whom I was like to give offence.[19]
Something there is that doesn't love a wall,
That wants it down." I could say "Elves" to him,
But it's not elves exactly, and I'd rather
He said it for himself. I see him there
Bringing a stone grasped firmly by the top
In each hand, like an old-stone savage armed.
He moves in darkness as it seems to me,[20]
Not of woods only and the shade of trees.
He will not go behind his father's saying,
And he likes having thought of it so well
He says again, "Good fences make good neighbours."

THE DEATH OF THE HIRED MAN

Mary sat musing on the lamp-flame at the table
Waiting for Warren. When she heard his step,
She ran on tip-toe down the darkened passage
To meet him in the doorway with the news
And put him on his guard. "Silas is back."
She pushed him outward with her through the door
And shut it after her. "Be kind," she said.
She took the market things from Warren's arms
And set them on the porch, then drew him down
To sit beside her on the wooden steps.

"When was I ever anything but kind to him?
But I'll not have the fellow back," he said.
"I told him so last haying, didn't I?
'If he left then,' I said, 'that ended it.'
What good is he? Who else will harbour him
At his age for the little he can do?
What help he is there's no depending on.
Off he goes always when I need him most.
He thinks he ought to earn a little pay,
Enough at least to buy tobacco with,
So he won't have to beg and be beholden.
'All right,' I say, 'I can't afford to pay
Any fixed wages, though I wish I could.'
'Someone else can.' 'Then someone else will have to.'
I shouldn't mind his bettering himself
If that was what it was. You can be certain,
When he begins like that, there's someone at him
Trying to coax him off with pocket-money,—

In haying time, when any help is scarce.
In winter he comes back to us. I'm done."

"Sh! not so loud: he'll hear you," Mary said.

"I want him to: he'll have to soon or late."

"He's worn out. He's asleep beside the stove.
When I came up from Rowe's I found him here,
Huddled against the barn-door fast asleep,
A miserable sight, and frightening, too—
You needn't smile—I didn't recognise him—
I wasn't looking for him—and he's changed.
Wait till you see."

                    "Where did you say he'd been?"

"He didn't say. I dragged him to the house,
And gave him tea and tried to make him smoke.
I tried to make him talk about his travels.
Nothing would do: he just kept nodding off."

"What did he say? Did he say anything?"

"But little."

                    "Anything? Mary, confess
He said he'd come to ditch the meadow for me."

"Warren!"

          "But did he? I just want to know."

"Of course he did. What would you have him say?

Surely you wouldn't grudge the poor old man
Some humble way to save his self-respect.
He added, if you really care to know,
He meant to clear the upper pasture, too.
That sounds like something you have heard before?
Warren, I wish you could have heard the way
He jumbled everything. I stopped to look
Two or three times—he made me feel so queer—
To see if he was talking in his sleep.
He ran on Harold Wilson—you remember—
The boy you had in haying four years since.
He's finished school, and teaching in his college.
Silas declares you'll have to get him back.
He says they two will make a team for work:
Between them they will lay this farm as smooth!
The way he mixed that in with other things.
He thinks young Wilson a likely lad, though daft
On education—you know how they fought
All through July under the blazing sun,
Silas up on the cart to build the load,
Harold along beside to pitch it on."

"Yes, I took care to keep well out of earshot."

"Well, those days trouble Silas like a dream.
You wouldn't think they would. How some things linger!
Harold's young college boy's assurance piqued him.
After so many years he still keeps finding
Good arguments he sees he might have used.
I sympathise. I know just how it feels
To think of the right thing to say too late.
Harold's associated in his mind with Latin.
He asked me what I thought of Harold's saying
He studied Latin like the violin

Because he liked it—that an argument!
He said he couldn't make the boy believe
He could find water with a hazel prong—
Which showed how much good school had ever done him.
He wanted to go over that. But most of all
He thinks if he could have another chance
To teach him how to build a load of hay—"

"I know, that's Silas' one accomplishment.
He bundles every forkful in its place,
And tags and numbers it for future reference,
So he can find and easily dislodge it
In the unloading. Silas does that well.
He takes it out in bunches like big birds' nests.
You never see him standing on the hay
He's trying to lift, straining to lift himself."

"He thinks if he could teach him that, he'd be
Some good perhaps to someone in the world.
He hates to see a boy the fool of books.
Poor Silas, so concerned for other folk,
And nothing to look backward to with pride,
And nothing to look forward to with hope,
So now and never any different."

Part of a moon was falling down the west,
Dragging the whole sky with it to the hills.
Its light poured softly in her lap. She saw
And spread her apron to it. She put out her hand
Among the harp-like morning-glory strings,
Taut with the dew from garden bed to eaves,
As if she played unheard the tenderness
That wrought on him beside her in the night.
"Warren," she said, "he has come home to die:

You needn't be afraid he'll leave you this time."

"Home," he mocked gently.

        "Yes, what else but home?
It all depends on what you mean by home.
Of course he's nothing to us, any more
Than was the hound that came a stranger to us
Out of the woods, worn out upon the trail."

"Home is the place where, when you have to go there,
They have to take you in."

        "I should have called it
Something you somehow haven't to deserve."

Warren leaned out and took a step or two,
Picked up a little stick, and brought it back
And broke it in his hand and tossed it by.
"Silas has better claim on us you think
Than on his brother? Thirteen little miles
As the road winds would bring him to his door.
Silas has walked that far no doubt to-day.
Why didn't he go there? His brother's rich,
A somebody—director in the bank."

"He never told us that."

        "We know it though."

"I think his brother ought to help, of course.
I'll see to that if there is need. He ought of right
To take him in, and might be willing to—
He may be better than appearances.

But have some pity on Silas. Do you think
If he'd had any pride in claiming kin
Or anything he looked for from his brother,
He'd keep so still about him all this time?"

"I wonder what's between them."

                        "I can tell you.
Silas is what he is—we wouldn't mind him—
But just the kind that kinsfolk can't abide.
He never did a thing so very bad.
He don't know why he isn't quite as good
As anyone. He won't be made ashamed
To please his brother, worthless though he is."

"*I* can't think Si ever hurt anyone."

"No, but he hurt my heart the way he lay
And rolled his old head on that sharp-edged chair-back.
He wouldn't let me put him on the lounge.
You must go in and see what you can do.
I made the bed up for him there to-night.
You'll be surprised at him—how much he's broken.
His working days are done; I'm sure of it."

"I'd not be in a hurry to say that."

"I haven't been. Go, look, see for yourself.
But, Warren, please remember how it is:
He's come to help you ditch the meadow.
He has a plan. You mustn't laugh at him.
He may not speak of it, and then he may.
I'll sit and see if that small sailing cloud
Will hit or miss the moon."

It hit the moon.
Then there were three there, making a dim row,
The moon, the little silver cloud, and she.

Warren returned—too soon, it seemed to her,
Slipped to her side, caught up her hand and waited.

"Warren?" she questioned.

      "Dead," was all he answered.

THE MOUNTAIN

The mountain held the town as in a shadow.[21]
I saw so much before I slept there once:
I noticed that I missed stars in the west,
Where its black body cut into the sky.
Near me it seemed: I felt it like a wall
Behind which I was sheltered from a wind.
And yet between the town and it I found,
When I walked forth at dawn to see new things,
Were fields, a river, and beyond, more fields.
The river at the time was fallen away,
And made a widespread brawl on cobble-stones;
But the signs showed what it had done in spring;
Good grass-land gullied out, and in the grass
Ridges of sand, and driftwood stripped of bark.
I crossed the river and swung round the mountain.
And there I met a man who moved so slow
With white-faced oxen in a heavy cart,
It seemed no harm to stop him altogether.

"What town is this?" I asked.

               "This? Lunenburg."[22]

Then I was wrong: the town of my sojourn,
Beyond the bridge, was not that of the mountain,
But only felt at night its shadowy presence.
"Where is your village? Very far from here?"

"There is no village—only scattered farms.
We were but sixty voters last election.
We can't in nature grow to many more:
That thing takes all the room!" He moved his goad.
The mountain stood there to be pointed at.
Pasture ran up the side a little way,
And then there was a wall of trees with trunks:
After that only tops of trees, and cliffs
Imperfectly concealed among the leaves.
A dry ravine emerged from under boughs
Into the pasture.

                    "That looks like a path.
Is that the way to reach the top from here?—
Not for this morning, but some other time:
I must be getting back to breakfast now."

"I don't advise your trying from this side.
There is no proper path, but those that *have*
Been up, I understand, have climbed from Ladd's.
That's five miles back. You can't mistake the place:
They logged it there last winter some way up.
I'd take you, but I'm bound the other way."

"You've never climbed it?"

                    "I've been on the sides
Deer-hunting and trout-fishing. There's a brook
That starts up on it somewhere—I've heard say
Right on the top, tip-top—a curious thing.
But what would interest you about the brook,
It's always cold in summer, warm in winter.
One of the great sights going is to see
It steam in winter like an ox's breath,

Until the bushes all along its banks
Are inch-deep with the frosty spines and bristles—
You know the kind. Then let the sun shine on it!"

"There ought to be a view around the world
From such a mountain—if it isn't wooded
Clear to the top." I saw through leafy screens
Great granite terraces in sun and shadow,
Shelves one could rest a knee on getting up—
With depths behind him sheer a hundred feet;
Or turn and sit on and look out and down,
With little ferns in crevices at his elbow.

"As to that I can't say. But there's the spring,
Right on the summit, almost like a fountain.
That ought to be worth seeing."

                              "If it's there.
You never saw it?"

                         "I guess there's no doubt
About its being there. I never saw it.
It may not be right on the very top:
It wouldn't have to be a long way down
To have some head of water from above,
And a *good distance* down might not be noticed
By anyone who'd come a long way up.
One time I asked a fellow climbing it
To look and tell me later how it was."

"What did he say?"

                         "He said there was a lake
Somewhere in Ireland on a mountain top."

"But a lake's different. What about the spring?"

"He never got up high enough to see.
 That's why I don't advise your trying this side.
 He tried this side. I've always meant to go
 And look myself, but you know how it is:
 It doesn't seem so much to climb a mountain
 You've worked around the foot of all your life.
 What would I do? Go in my overalls,
 With a big stick, the same as when the cows
 Haven't come down to the bars at milking time?
 Or with a shotgun for a stray black bear?
 'Twouldn't seem real to climb for climbing it."

"I shouldn't climb it if I didn't want to—
 Not for the sake of climbing. What's its name?"

"We call it Hor: I don't know if that's right."[23]

"Can one walk around it? Would it be too far?"

"You can drive round and keep in Lunenburg,
 But it's as much as ever you can do,
 The boundary lines keep in so close to it.
 Hor is the township, and the township's Hor—
 And a few houses sprinkled round the foot,
 Like boulders broken off the upper cliff,
 Rolled out a little farther than the rest."

"Warm in December, cold in June, you say?"

"I don't suppose the water's changed at all.
 You and I know enough to know it's warm
 Compared with cold, and cold compared with warm.

But all the fun's in how you say a thing."

"You've lived here all your life?"

                                "Ever since Hor
Was no bigger than a——" What, I did not hear.
He drew the oxen toward him with light touches
Of his slim goad on nose and offside flank,
Gave them their marching orders and was moving.

A HUNDRED COLLARS

Lancaster bore him—such a little town,
Such a great man. It doesn't see him often
Of late years, though he keeps the old homestead
And sends the children down there with their mother
To run wild in the summer—a little wild.
Sometimes he joins them for a day or two
And sees old friends he somehow can't get near.
They meet him in the general store at night,
Pre-occupied with formidable mail,
Rifling a printed letter as he talks.
They seem afraid. He wouldn't have it so:
Though a great scholar, he's a democrat,
If not at heart, at least on principle.
Lately when coming up to Lancaster
His train being late he missed another train
And had four hours to wait at Woodsville Junction
After eleven o'clock at night. Too tired
To think of sitting such an ordeal out,
He turned to the hotel to find a bed.

"No room," the night clerk said. "Unless——"
Woodsville's a place of shrieks and wandering lamps
And cars that shock and rattle—and *one* hotel.

"You say 'unless.'"

                    "Unless you wouldn't mind
Sharing a room with someone else."

"Who is it?"

"A man."

"So I should hope. What kind of man?"

"I know him: he's all right. A man's a man.
Separate beds of course you understand."
The night clerk blinked his eyes and dared him on.

"Who's that man sleeping in the office chair?
Has he had the refusal of my chance?"

"He was afraid of being robbed or murdered.
What do you say?"

                    "I'll have to have a bed."

The night clerk led him up three flights of stairs
And down a narrow passage full of doors,
At the last one of which he knocked and entered.
"Lafe, here's a fellow wants to share your room."

"Show him this way. I'm not afraid of him.
I'm not so drunk I can't take care of myself."

The night clerk clapped a bedstead on the foot.
"This will be yours. Good-night," he said, and went.

"Lafe was the name, I think?"

                    "Yes, *Lay*fayette.
You got it the first time. And yours?"

"Magoon.
Doctor Magoon."

            "A Doctor?"

                    "Well, a teacher."

"Professor Square-the-circle-till-you're-tired?
Hold on, there's something I don't think of now
That I had on my mind to ask the first
Man that knew anything I happened in with.
I'll ask you later—don't let me forget it."

The Doctor looked at Lafe and looked away.
A man? A brute. Naked above the waist,
He sat there creased and shining in the light,
Fumbling the buttons in a well-starched shirt.
"I'm moving into a size-larger shirt.
I've felt mean lately; mean's no name for it.
I just found what the matter was to-night:
I've been a-choking like a nursery tree
When it outgrows the wire band of its name tag.
I blamed it on the hot spell we've been having.
'Twas nothing but my foolish hanging back,
Not liking to own up I'd grown a size.
Number eighteen this is. What size do you wear?"

The Doctor caught his throat convulsively.
"Oh—ah—fourteen—fourteen."

                    "Fourteen! You say so!
I can remember when I wore fourteen.
And come to think I must have back at home
More than a hundred collars, size fourteen.

Too bad to waste them all. You ought to have them.
They're yours and welcome; let me send them to you.
What makes you stand there on one leg like that?
You're not much furtherer than where Kike left you.
You act as if you wished you hadn't come.
Sit down or lie down, friend; you make me nervous."

The Doctor made a subdued dash for it,
And propped himself at bay against a pillow.

"Not that way, with your shoes on Kike's white bed.
You can't rest that way. Let me pull your shoes off."

"Don't touch me, please—I say, don't touch me, please.
I'll not be put to bed by you, my man."

"Just as you say. Have it your own way then.
'My man' is it? You talk like a professor.
Speaking of who's afraid of who, however,
I'm thinking I have more to lose than you
If anything should happen to be wrong.
Who wants to cut your number fourteen throat!
Let's have a show down as an evidence
Of good faith. There is ninety dollars.
Come, if you're not afraid."

                              "I'm not afraid.
There's five: that's all I carry."

                              "I can search you?
Where are you moving over to? Stay still.
You'd better tuck your money under you
And sleep on it the way I always do
When I'm with people I don't trust at night."

"Will you believe me if I put it there
  Right on the counterpane—that I do trust you?"

"You'd say so, Mister Man.—I'm a collector.
  My ninety isn't mine—you won't think that.
  I pick it up a dollar at a time
  All round the country for the *Weekly News,*
  Published in Bow. You know the *Weekly News?*"

"Known it since I was young."

                                    "Then you know me.
  Now we are getting on together—talking.
  I'm sort of Something for it at the front.
  My business is to find what people want:
  They pay for it, and so they ought to have it.
  Fairbanks, he says to me—he's editor—
  Feel out the public sentiment—he says.
  A good deal comes on me when all is said.
  The only trouble is we disagree
  In politics: I'm Vermont Democrat—[24]
  You know what that is, sort of double-dyed;
  The *News* has always been Republican.
  Fairbanks, he says to me, 'Help us this year,'
  Meaning by us their ticket. 'No,' I says,
  'I can't and won't. You've been in long enough:
  It's time you turned around and boosted us.
  You'll have to pay me more than ten a week
  If I'm expected to elect Bill Taft.[25]
  I doubt if I could do it anyway.'"

"You seem to shape the paper's policy."

"You see I'm in with everybody, know 'em all.
I almost know their farms as well as they do."

"You drive around? It must be pleasant work."

"It's business, but I can't say it's not fun.
What I like best's the lay of different farms,
Coming out on them from a stretch of woods,
Or over a hill or round a sudden corner.
I like to find folks getting out in spring,
Raking the dooryard, working near the house.
Later they get out further in the fields.
Everything's shut sometimes except the barn;
The family's all away in some back meadow.
There's a hay load a-coming—when it comes.
And later still they all get driven in:
The fields are stripped to lawn, the garden patches
Stripped to bare ground, the apple trees
To whips and poles. There's nobody about.
The chimney, though, keeps up a good brisk smoking.
And I lie back and ride. I take the reins
Only when someone's coming, and the mare
Stops when she likes: I tell her when to go.
I've spoiled Jemima in more ways than one.
She's got so she turns in at every house
As if she had some sort of curvature,
No matter if I have no errand there.
She thinks I'm sociable. I maybe am.
It's seldom I get down except for meals, though.
Folks entertain me from the kitchen doorstep,
All in a family row down to the youngest."

"One would suppose they might not be as glad
   To see you as you are to see them."

                              "Oh,
Because I want their dollar. I don't want
Anything they've not got. I never dun.
I'm there, and they can pay me if they like.
I go nowhere on purpose: I happen by.
Sorry there is no cup to give you a drink.
I drink out of the bottle—not your style.
Mayn't I offer you——?"

            "No, no, no, thank you."

"Just as you say. Here's looking at you then.—
And now I'm leaving you a little while.
You'll rest easier when I'm gone, perhaps—
Lie down—let yourself go and get some sleep.
But first—let's see—what was I going to ask you?
Those collars—who shall I address them to,
Suppose you aren't awake when I come back?"

"Really, friend, I can't let you. You—may need them."

"Not till I shrink, when they'll be out of style."

"But really I—I have so many collars."

"I don't know who I rather would have have them.
 They're only turning yellow where they are.
 But you're the doctor as the saying is.
 I'll put the light out. Don't you wait for me:
 I've just begun the night. You get some sleep.
 I'll knock so-fashion and peep round the door
 When I come back so you'll know who it is.
 There's nothing I'm afraid of like scared people.
 I don't want you should shoot me in the head.

What am I doing carrying off this bottle?
There now, you get some sleep."

He shut the door.
The Doctor slid a little down the pillow.

HOME BURIAL

He saw her from the bottom of the stairs
Before she saw him. She was starting down,
Looking back over her shoulder at some fear.
She took a doubtful step and then undid it
To raise herself and look again. He spoke
Advancing toward her: "What is it you see
From up there always—for I want to know."
She turned and sank upon her skirts at that,
And her face changed from terrified to dull.
He said to gain time: "What is it you see,"
Mounting until she cowered under him.
"I will find out now—you must tell me, dear."
She, in her place, refused him any help
With the least stiffening of her neck and silence.
She let him look, sure that he wouldn't see,
Blind creature; and a while he didn't see.
But at last he murmured, "Oh," and again, "Oh."

"What is it—what?" she said.

                    "Just that I see."

"You don't," she challenged. "Tell me what it is."

"The wonder is I didn't see at once.
I never noticed it from here before.
I must be wonted to it—that's the reason.
The little graveyard where my people are!
So small the window frames the whole of it.

Not so much larger than a bedroom, is it?
There are three stones of slate and one of marble,
Broad-shouldered little slabs there in the sunlight
On the sidehill. We haven't to mind *those.*
But I understand: it is not the stones,
But the child's mound—"

"Don't, don't, don't, don't," she cried.

She withdrew shrinking from beneath his arm
That rested on the banister, and slid downstairs;
And turned on him with such a daunting look,
He said twice over before he knew himself:
"Can't a man speak of his own child he's lost?"

"Not you! Oh, where's my hat? Oh, I don't need it!
I must get out of here. I must get air.
I don't know rightly whether any man can."

"Amy! Don't go to someone else this time.
Listen to me. I won't come down the stairs."
He sat and fixed his chin between his fists.
"There's something I should like to ask you, dear."

"You don't know how to ask it."

"Help me, then."
Her fingers moved the latch for all reply.

"My words are nearly always an offence.
I don't know how to speak of anything
So as to please you. But I might be taught
I should suppose. I can't say I see how.
A man must partly give up being a man

With women-folk. We could have some arrangement
By which I'd bind myself to keep hands off
Anything special you're a-mind to name.
Though I don't like such things 'twixt those that love.
Two that don't love can't live together without them.
But two that do can't live together with them."
She moved the latch a little. "Don't—don't go.
Don't carry it to someone else this time.
Tell me about it if it's something human.
Let me into your grief. I'm not so much
Unlike other folks as your standing there
Apart would make me out. Give me my chance.
I do think, though, you overdo it a little.
What was it brought you up to think it the thing
To take your mother-loss of a first child
So inconsolably—in the face of love.
You'd think his memory might be satisfied——"

"There you go sneering now!"

        "I'm not, I'm not!
You make me angry. I'll come down to you.
God, what a woman! And it's come to this,
A man can't speak of his own child that's dead."

"You can't because you don't know how.
If you had any feelings, you that dug
With your own hand—how could you?—his little grave;
I saw you from that very window there,
Making the gravel leap and leap in air,
Leap up, like that, like that, and land so lightly
And roll back down the mound beside the hole.
I thought, Who is that man? I didn't know you.
And I crept down the stairs and up the stairs

To look again, and still your spade kept lifting.
Then you came in. I heard your rumbling voice
Out in the kitchen, and I don't know why,
But I went near to see with my own eyes.
You could sit there with the stains on your shoes
Of the fresh earth from your own baby's grave
And talk about your everyday concerns.
You had stood the spade up against the wall
Outside there in the entry, for I saw it."

"I shall laugh the worst laugh I ever laughed.
I'm cursed. God, if I don't believe I'm cursed."

"I can repeat the very words you were saying.
'Three foggy mornings and one rainy day
Will rot the best birch fence a man can build.'
Think of it, talk like that at such a time!
What had how long it takes a birch to rot
To do with what was in the darkened parlour.
You *couldn't* care! The nearest friends can go
With anyone to death, comes so far short
They might as well not try to go at all.
No, from the time when one is sick to death,
One is alone, and he dies more alone.
Friends make pretence of following to the grave,
But before one is in it, their minds are turned
And making the best of their way back to life
And living people, and things they understand.
But the world's evil. I won't have grief so
If I can change it. Oh, I won't, I won't!"

"There, you have said it all and you feel better.
 You won't go now. You're crying. Close the door.
 The heart's gone out of it: why keep it up.
 Amy! There's someone coming down the road!"

"*You*—oh, you think the talk is all. I must go—
 Somewhere out of this house. How can I make you——"

"If—you—do!" She was opening the door wider.
"Where do you mean to go? First tell me that.
 I'll follow and bring you back by force. I *will!*—"

THE BLACK COTTAGE

We chanced in passing by that afternoon
To catch it in a sort of special picture
Among tar-banded ancient cherry trees,
Set well back from the road in rank lodged grass,
The little cottage we were speaking of,
A front with just a door between two windows,
Fresh painted by the shower a velvet black.
We paused, the minister and I, to look.
He made as if to hold it at arm's length
Or put the leaves aside that framed it in.
"Pretty," he said. "Come in. No one will care."
The path was a vague parting in the grass
That led us to a weathered window-sill.
We pressed our faces to the pane. "You see," he said,
"Everything's as she left it when she died.
Her sons won't sell the house or the things in it.
They say they mean to come and summer here
Where they were boys. They haven't come this year.
They live so far away—one is out west—
It will be hard for them to keep their word.
Anyway they won't have the place disturbed."
A buttoned hair-cloth lounge spread scrolling arms
Under a crayon portrait on the wall
Done sadly from an old daguerreotype.
"That was the father as he went to war.
She always, when she talked about war,
Sooner or later came and leaned, half knelt
Against the lounge beside it, though I doubt
If such unlifelike lines kept power to stir

Anything in her after all the years.
He fell at Gettysburg or Fredericksburg,[26]
I ought to know—it makes a difference which:
Fredericksburg wasn't Gettysburg, of course.
But what I'm getting to is how forsaken
A little cottage this has always seemed;
Since she went more than ever, but before—
I don't mean altogether by the lives
That had gone out of it, the father first,
Then the two sons, till she was left alone.
(Nothing could draw her after those two sons.
She valued the considerate neglect
She had at some cost taught them after years.)
I mean by the world's having passed it by—
As we almost got by this afternoon.
It always seems to me a sort of mark
To measure how far fifty years have brought us.
Why not sit down if you are in no haste?
These doorsteps seldom have a visitor.
The warping boards pull out their own old nails
With none to tread and put them in their place.
She had her own idea of things, the old lady.
And she liked talk. She had seen Garrison[27]
And Whittier, and had her story of them.[28]
One wasn't long in learning that she thought
Whatever else the Civil War was for
It wasn't just to keep the States together,
Nor just to free the slaves, though it did both.
She wouldn't have believed those ends enough
To have given outright for them all she gave.
Her giving somehow touched the principle
That all men are created free and equal.[29]
And to hear her quaint phrases—so removed
From the world's view to-day of all those things.

That's a hard mystery of Jefferson's.
What did he mean? Of course the easy way
Is to decide it simply isn't true.
It may not be. I heard a fellow say so.
But never mind, the Welshman got it planted[30]
Where it will trouble us a thousand years.
Each age will have to reconsider it.
You couldn't tell her what the West was saying.
And what the South to her serene belief.
She had some art of hearing and yet not
Hearing the latter wisdom of the world.
White was the only race she ever knew.
Black she had scarcely seen, and yellow never.
But how could they be made so very unlike
By the same hand working in the same stuff?
She had supposed the war decided that.
What are you going to do with such a person?
Strange how such innocence gets its own way.
I shouldn't be surprised if in this world
It were the force that would at last prevail.
Do you know but for her there was a time
When to please younger members of the church,
Or rather say non-members in the church,
Whom we all have to think of nowadays,
I would have changed the Creed a very little?[31]
Not that she ever had to ask me not to;
It never got so far as that; but the bare thought
Of her old tremulous bonnet in the pew,
And of her half asleep was too much for me.
Why, I might wake her up and startle her.
It was the words 'descended into Hades'[32]
That seemed too pagan to our liberal youth.
You know they suffered from a general onslaught.
And well, if they weren't true why keep right on

Saying them like the heathen? We could drop them.
Only—there was the bonnet in the pew.
Such a phrase couldn't have meant much to her.
But suppose she had missed it from the Creed
As a child misses the unsaid Good-night,
And falls asleep with heartache—how should *I* feel?
I'm just as glad she made me keep hands off,
For, dear me, why abandon a belief
Merely because it ceases to be true.
Cling to it long enough, and not a doubt
It will turn true again, for so it goes.
Most of the change we think we see in life
Is due to truths being in and out of favour.
As I sit here, and oftentimes, I wish
I could be monarch of a desert land
I could devote and dedicate forever
To the truths we keep coming back and back to.
So desert it would have to be, so walled
By mountain ranges half in summer snow,
No one would covet it or think it worth
The pains of conquering to force change on.
Scattered oases where men dwelt, but mostly
Sand dunes held loosely in tamarisk
Blown over and over themselves in idleness.
Sand grains should sugar in the natal dew
The babe born to the desert, the sand storm
Retard mid-waste my cowering caravans—

"There are bees in this wall." He struck the clapboards,
Fierce heads looked out; small bodies pivoted.
We rose to go. Sunset blazed on the windows.

BLUEBERRIES

"You ought to have seen what I saw on my way
  To the village, through Mortenson's pasture to-day:
  Blueberries as big as the end of your thumb,
  Real sky-blue, and heavy, and ready to drum
  In the cavernous pail of the first one to come!
  And all ripe together, not some of them green
  And some of them ripe! You ought to have seen!"

"I don't know what part of the pasture you mean."

"You know where they cut off the woods—let me see—
  It was two years ago—or no!—can it be
  No longer than that?—and the following fall
  The fire ran and burned it all up but the wall."

"Why, there hasn't been time for the bushes to grow.
  That's always the way with the blueberries, though:
  There may not have been the ghost of a sign
  Of them anywhere under the shade of the pine,
  But get the pine out of the way, you may burn
  The pasture all over until not a fern
  Or grass-blade is left, not to mention a stick,
  And presto, they're up all around you as thick
  And hard to explain as a conjuror's trick."

"It must be on charcoal they fatten their fruit.
  I taste in them sometimes the flavour of soot.
  And after all really they're ebony skinned:
  The blue's but a mist from the breath of the wind,

A tarnish that goes at a touch of the hand,
And less than the tan with which pickers are tanned."

"Does Mortenson know what he has, do you think?"

"He may and not care and so leave the chewink[33]
To gather them for him—you know what he is.
He won't make the fact that they're rightfully his
An excuse for keeping us other folk out."

"I wonder you didn't see Loren about."

"The best of it was that I did. Do you know,
I was just getting through what the field had to show
And over the wall and into the road,
When who should come by, with a democrat-load
Of all the young chattering Lorens alive,
But Loren, the fatherly, out for a drive."

"He saw you, then? What did he do? Did he frown?"

"He just kept nodding his head up and down.
You know how politely he always goes by.
But he thought a big thought—I could tell by his eye—
Which being expressed, might be this in effect:
'I have left those there berries, I shrewdly suspect,
To ripen too long. I am greatly to blame.'"

"He's a thriftier person than some I could name."

"He seems to be thrifty; and hasn't he need,
With the mouths of all those young Lorens to feed?
He has brought them all up on wild berries, they say,
Like birds. They store a great many away.

They eat them the year round, and those they don't eat
They sell in the store and buy shoes for their feet."

"Who cares what they say? It's a nice way to live,
Just taking what Nature is willing to give,
Not forcing her hand with harrow and plow."

"I wish you had seen his perpetual bow—
And the air of the youngsters! Not one of them turned,
And they looked so solemn-absurdly concerned."

"I wish I knew half what the flock of them know
Of where all the berries and other things grow,
Cranberries in bogs and raspberries on top
Of the boulder-strewn mountain, and when they will crop.
I met them one day and each had a flower
Stuck into his berries as fresh as a shower;
Some strange kind—they told me it hadn't a name."

"I've told you how once not long after we came,
I almost provoked poor Loren to mirth
By going to him of all people on earth
To ask if he knew any fruit to be had
For the picking. The rascal, he said he'd be glad
To tell if he knew. But the year had been bad.
There *had* been some berries—but those were all gone.
He didn't say where they had been. He went on:
'I'm sure—I'm sure'—as polite as could be.
He spoke to his wife in the door, 'Let me see,
Mame, *we* don't know any good berrying place?'
It was all he could do to keep a straight face."

"If he thinks all the fruit that grows wild is for him,
He'll find he's mistaken. See here, for a whim,

We'll pick in the Mortensons' pasture this year.
We'll go in the morning, that is, if it's clear,
And the sun shines out warm: the vines must be wet.
It's so long since I picked I almost forget
How we used to pick berries: we took one look round,
Then sank out of sight like trolls underground,
And saw nothing more of each other, or heard,
Unless when you said I was keeping a bird
Away from its nest, and I said it was you.
'Well, one of us is.' For complaining it flew
Around and around us. And then for a while
We picked, till I feared you had wandered a mile,
And I thought I had lost you. I lifted a shout
Too loud for the distance you were, it turned out,
For when you made answer, your voice was as low
As talking—you stood up beside me, you know."

"We sha'n't have the place to ourselves to enjoy—
Not likely, when all the young Lorens deploy.
They'll be there to-morrow, or even to-night.
They won't be too friendly—they may be polite—
To people they look on as having no right
To pick where they're picking. But we won't complain.
You ought to have seen how it looked in the rain,
The fruit mixed with water in layers of leaves,
Like two kinds of jewels, a vision for thieves."

A SERVANT TO SERVANTS[34]

I didn't make you know how glad I was
To have you come and camp here on our land.
I promised myself to get down some day
And see the way you lived, but I don't know!
With a houseful of hungry men to feed
I guess you'd find. . . . It seems to me
I can't express my feelings any more
Than I can raise my voice or want to lift
My hand (oh, I can lift it when I have to).
Did ever you feel so? I hope you never.
It's got so I don't even know for sure
Whether I *am* glad, sorry, or anything.
There's nothing but a voice-like left inside
That seems to tell me how I ought to feel,
And would feel if I wasn't all gone wrong.
You take the lake. I look and look at it.
I see it's a fair, pretty sheet of water.
I stand and make myself repeat out loud
The advantages it has, so long and narrow,
Like a deep piece of some old running river
Cut short off at both ends. It lies five miles
Straight away through the mountain notch
From the sink window where I wash the plates,
And all our storms come up toward the house,
Drawing the slow waves whiter and whiter and whiter.
It took my mind off doughnuts and soda biscuit
To step outdoors and take the water dazzle
A sunny morning, or take the rising wind
About my face and body and through my wrapper,

When a storm threatened from the Dragon's Den,
And a cold chill shivered across the lake.
I see it's a fair, pretty sheet of water,
Our Willoughby! How did you hear of it?[35]
I expect, though, everyone's heard of it.
In a book about ferns? Listen to that!
You let things more like feathers regulate
Your going and coming. And you like it here?
I can see how you might. But I don't know!
It would be different if more people came,
For then there would be business. As it is,
The cottages Len built, sometimes we rent them,
Sometimes we don't. We've a good piece of shore
That ought to be worth something, and may yet.
But I don't count on it as much as Len.
He looks on the bright side of everything,
Including me. He thinks I'll be all right
With doctoring. But it's not medicine—
Lowe is the only doctor's dared to say so—
It's rest I want—there, I have said it out—
From cooking meals for hungry hired men
And washing dishes after them—from doing
Things over and over that just won't stay done.
By good rights I ought not to have so much
Put on me, but there seems no other way.
Len says one steady pull more ought to do it.
He says the best way out is always through.
And I agree to that, or in so far
As that I can see no way out but through—
Leastways for me—and then they'll be convinced.
It's not that Len don't want the best for me.
It was his plan our moving over in
Beside the lake from where that day I showed you
We used to live—ten miles from anywhere.

We didn't change without some sacrifice,
But Len went at it to make up the loss.
His work's a man's, of course, from sun to sun,
But he works when he works as hard as I do—
Though there's small profit in comparisons.
(Women and men will make them all the same.)
But work ain't all. Len undertakes too much.
He's into everything in town. This year
It's highways, and he's got too many men
Around him to look after that make waste.
They take advantage of him shamefully,
And proud, too, of themselves for doing so.
We have four here to board, great good-for-nothings,
Sprawling about the kitchen with their talk
While I fry their bacon. Much they care!
No more put out in what they do or say
Than if I wasn't in the room at all.
Coming and going all the time, they are:
I don't learn what their names are, let alone
Their characters, or whether they are safe
To have inside the house with doors unlocked.
I'm not afraid of them, though, if they're not
Afraid of me. There's two can play at that.
I have my fancies: it runs in the family.
My father's brother wasn't right. They kept him
Locked up for years back there at the old farm.
I've been away once—yes, I've been away.
The State Asylum. I was prejudiced;
I wouldn't have sent anyone of mine there;
You know the old idea—the only asylum
Was the poorhouse, and those who could afford,
Rather than send their folks to such a place,
Kept them at home; and it does seem more human.
But it's not so: the place is the asylum.

There they have every means proper to do with,
And you aren't darkening other people's lives—
Worse than no good to them, and they no good
To you in your condition; you can't know
Affection or the want of it in that state.
I've heard too much of the old-fashioned way.
My father's brother, he went mad quite young.
Some thought he had been bitten by a dog,
Because his violence took on the form
Of carrying his pillow in his teeth;
But it's more likely he was crossed in love,
Or so the story goes. It was some girl.
Anyway all he talked about was love.
They soon saw he would do someone a mischief
If he wa'n't kept strict watch of, and it ended
In father's building him a sort of cage,
Or room within a room, of hickory poles,
Like stanchions in the barn, from floor to ceiling,—
A narrow passage all the way around.
Anything they put in for furniture
He'd tear to pieces, even a bed to lie on.
So they made the place comfortable with straw,
Like a beast's stall, to ease their consciences.
Of course they had to feed him without dishes.
They tried to keep him clothed, but he paraded
With his clothes on his arm—all of his clothes.
Cruel—it sounds. I s'pose they did the best
They knew. And just when he was at the height,
Father and mother married, and mother came,
A bride, to help take care of such a creature,
And accommodate her young life to his.
That was what marrying father meant to her.
She had to lie and hear love things made dreadful
By his shouts in the night. He'd shout and shout

Until the strength was shouted out of him,
And his voice died down slowly from exhaustion.
He'd pull his bars apart like bow and bowstring,
And let them go and make them twang until
His hands had worn them smooth as any oxbow.
And then he'd crow as if he thought that child's play—
The only fun he had. I've heard them say, though,
They found a way to put a stop to it.
He was before my time—I never saw him;
But the pen stayed exactly as it was
There in the upper chamber in the ell,
A sort of catch-all full of attic clutter.
I often think of the smooth hickory bars.
It got so I would say—you know, half fooling—
"It's time I took my turn upstairs in jail"—
Just as you will till it becomes a habit.
No wonder I was glad to get away.
Mind you, I waited till Len said the word.
I didn't want the blame if things went wrong.
I was glad though, no end, when we moved out,
And I looked to be happy, and I was,
As I said, for a while—but I don't know!
Somehow the change wore out like a prescription.
And there's more to it than just window-views
And living by a lake. I'm past such help—
Unless Len took the notion, which he won't,
And I won't ask him—it's not sure enough.
I s'pose I've got to go the road I'm going:
Other folks have to, and why shouldn't I?
I almost think if I could do like you,
Drop everything and live out on the ground—
But it might be, come night, I shouldn't like it,
Or a long rain. I should soon get enough,
And be glad of a good roof overhead.

I've lain awake thinking of you, I'll warrant,
More than you have yourself, some of these nights.
The wonder was the tents weren't snatched away
From over you as you lay in your beds.
I haven't courage for a risk like that.
Bless you, of course, you're keeping me from work,
But the thing of it is, I need to *be* kept.
There's work enough to do—there's always that;
But behind's behind. The worst that you can do
Is set me back a little more behind.
I shan't catch up in this world, anyway.
I'd *rather* you'd not go unless you must.

AFTER APPLE-PICKING

My long two-pointed ladder's sticking through a tree
Toward heaven still,
And there's a barrel that I didn't fill
Beside it, and there may be two or three
Apples I didn't pick upon some bough.
But I am done with apple-picking now.
Essence of winter sleep is on the night,
The scent of apples: I am drowsing off.
I cannot rub the strangeness from my sight[36]
I got from looking through a pane of glass
I skimmed this morning from the drinking trough
And held against the world of hoary grass.
It melted, and I let it fall and break.
But I was well
Upon my way to sleep before it fell,
And I could tell
What form my dreaming was about to take.
Magnified apples appear and disappear,
Stem end and blossom end,
And every fleck of russet showing clear.
My instep arch not only keeps the ache,
It keeps the pressure of a ladder-round.
I feel the ladder sway as the boughs bend.
And I keep hearing from the cellar bin
The rumbling sound
Of load on load of apples coming in.
For I have had too much
Of apple-picking: I am overtired
Of the great harvest I myself desired.

There were ten thousand thousand fruit to touch,
Cherish in hand, lift down, and not let fall.
For all
That struck the earth,
No matter if not bruised or spiked with stubble,
Went surely to the cider-apple heap
As of no worth.
One can see what will trouble
This sleep of mine, whatever sleep it is.
Were he not gone,
The woodchuck could say whether it's like his
Long sleep, as I describe its coming on,
Or just some human sleep.

THE CODE

There were three in the meadow by the brook
Gathering up windrows, piling cocks of hay,
With an eye always lifted toward the west
Where an irregular sun-bordered cloud
Darkly advanced with a perpetual dagger
Flickering across its bosom. Suddenly
One helper, thrusting pitchfork in the ground,
Marched himself off the field and home. One stayed.
The town-bred farmer failed to understand.

"What is there wrong?"

        "Something you just now said."

"What did I say?"

        "About our taking pains."

"To cock the hay?—because it's going to shower?
I said that more than half an hour ago.
I said it to myself as much as you."

"You didn't know. But James is one big fool.
He thought you meant to find fault with his work.
That's what the average farmer would have meant.
James would take time, of course, to chew it over
Before he acted: he's just got round to act."

"He is a fool if that's the way he takes me."

"Don't let it bother you. You've found out something.
The hand that knows his business won't be told
To do work better or faster—those two things.
I'm as particular as anyone:
Most likely I'd have served you just the same.
But I know you don't understand our ways.
You were just talking what was in your mind,
What was in all our minds, and you weren't hinting.
Tell you a story of what happened once:
I was up here in Salem at a man's[37]
Named Sanders with a gang of four or five
Doing the haying. No one liked the boss.
He was one of the kind sports call a spider,
All wiry arms and legs that spread out wavy
From a humped body nigh as big's a biscuit.
But work! that man could work, especially
If by so doing he could get more work
Out of his hired help. I'm not denying
He was hard on himself. I couldn't find
That he kept any hours—not for himself.
Daylight and lantern-light were one to him:
I've heard him pounding in the barn all night.
But what he liked was someone to encourage.
Them that he couldn't lead he'd get behind
And drive, the way you can, you know, in mowing—
Keep at their heels and threaten to mow their legs off.
I'd seen about enough of his bulling tricks[38]
(We call that bulling). I'd been watching him.
So when he paired off with me in the hayfield
To load the load, thinks I, Look out for trouble.
I built the load and topped it off; old Sanders
Combed it down with a rake and says, 'O. K.'
Everything went well till we reached the barn
With a big catch to empty in a bay.

You understand that meant the easy job
For the man up on top of throwing *down*
The hay and rolling it off wholesale,
Where on a mow it would have been slow lifting.
You wouldn't think a fellow'd need much urging
Under these circumstances, would you now?
But the old fool seizes his fork in both hands,
And looking up bewhiskered out of the pit,
Shouts like an army captain, 'Let her come!'
Thinks I, D'ye mean it? 'What was that you said?'
I asked out loud, so's there'd be no mistake,
'Did you say, Let her come?' 'Yes, let her come.'
He said it over, but he said it softer.
Never you say a thing like that to a man,
Not if he values what he is. God, I'd as soon
Murdered him as left out his middle name.
I'd built the load and knew right where to find it.
Two or three forkfuls I picked lightly round for
Like meditating, and then I just dug in
And dumped the rackful on him in ten lots.
I looked over the side once in the dust
And caught sight of him treading-water-like,
Keeping his head above. 'Damn ye,' I says,
'That gets ye!' He squeaked like a squeezed rat.
That was the last I saw or heard of him.
I cleaned the rack and drove out to cool off.
As I sat mopping hayseed from my neck,
And sort of waiting to be asked about it,
One of the boys sings out, 'Where's the old man?'
'I left him in the barn under the hay.
If ye want him, ye can go and dig him out.'
They realized from the way I swabbed my neck
More than was needed something must be up.
They headed for the barn; I stayed where I was.

They told me afterward. First they forked hay,
A lot of it, out into the barn floor.
Nothing! They listened for him. Not a rustle.
I guess they thought I'd spiked him in the temple
Before I buried him, or I couldn't have managed.
They excavated more. 'Go keep his wife
Out of the barn.' Someone looked in a window,
And curse me if he wasn't in the kitchen
Slumped way down in a chair, with both his feet
Stuck in the oven, the hottest day that summer.
He looked so clean disgusted from behind
There was no one that dared to stir him up,
Or let him know that he was being looked at.
Apparently I hadn't buried him
(I may have knocked him down); but my just trying
To bury him had hurt his dignity.
He had gone to the house so's not to meet me.
He kept away from us all afternoon.
We tended to his hay. We saw him out
After a while picking peas in his garden:
He couldn't keep away from doing something."

"Weren't you relieved to find he wasn't dead?"

"No! and yet I don't know—it's hard to say.
I went about to kill him fair enough."

"You took an awkward way. Did he discharge you?"

"Discharge me? No! He knew I did just right."

THE GENERATIONS OF MEN

A governor it was proclaimed this time,
When all who would come seeking in New Hampshire
Ancestral memories might come together.
And those of the name Stark gathered in Bow,[39]
A rock-strewn town where farming has fallen off,
And sprout-lands flourish where the axe has gone.
Someone had literally run to earth
In an old cellar hole in a by-road
The origin of all the family there.
Thence they were sprung, so numerous a tribe
That now not all the houses left in town
Made shift to shelter them without the help
Of here and there a tent in grove and orchard.
They were at Bow, but that was not enough:
Nothing would do but they must fix a day
To stand together on the crater's verge
That turned them on the world, and try to fathom
The past and get some strangeness out of it.
But rain spoiled all. The day began uncertain,
With clouds low trailing and moments of rain that misted.
The young folk held some hope out to each other
Till well toward noon when the storm settled down
With a swish in the grass. "What if the others
Are there," they said. "It isn't going to rain."
Only one from a farm not far away
Strolled thither, not expecting he would find
Anyone else, but out of idleness.
One, and one other, yes, for there were two.
The second round the curving hillside road

Was a girl; and she halted some way off
To reconnoitre, and then made up her mind
At least to pass by and see who he was,
And perhaps hear some word about the weather.
This was some Stark she didn't know. He nodded.
"No fête to-day," he said.

                    "It looks that way."

She swept the heavens, turning on her heel.
"I only idled down."

              "I idled down."

Provision there had been for just such meeting
Of stranger cousins, in a family tree
Drawn on a sort of passport with the branch
Of the one bearing it done in detail—
Some zealous one's laborious device.
She made a sudden movement toward her bodice,
As one who clasps her heart. They laughed together.
"Stark?" he inquired. "No matter for the proof."

"Yes, Stark. And you?"

              "I'm Stark." He drew his passport.

"You know we might not be and still be cousins:
The town is full of Chases, Lowes, and Baileys,
All claiming some priority in Starkness.
My mother was a Lane, yet might have married
Anyone upon earth and still her children
Would have been Starks, and doubtless here to-day."

"You riddle with your genealogy[40]
Like a Viola. I don't follow you."

"I only mean my mother was a Stark
Several times over, and by marrying father
No more than brought us back into the name."

"One ought not to be thrown into confusion
By a plain statement of relationship,
But I own what you say makes my head spin.
You take my card—you seem so good at such things—
And see if you can reckon our cousinship.
Why not take seats here on the cellar wall
And dangle feet among the raspberry vines?"

"Under the shelter of the family tree."

"Just so—that ought to be enough protection."

"Not from the rain. I think it's going to rain."

"It's raining."

       "No, it's misting; let's be fair.
Does the rain seem to you to cool the eyes?"

The situation was like this: the road
Bowed outward on the mountain half-way up,
And disappeared and ended not far off.
No one went home that way. The only house
Beyond where they were was a shattered seedpod.
And below roared a brook hidden in trees,
The sound of which was silence for the place.
This he sat listening to till she gave judgment.

"On father's side, it seems, we're—let me see——"

"Don't be too technical.—You have three cards."

"Four cards, one yours, three mine, one for each branch
  Of the Stark family I'm a member of."

"D'you know a person so related to herself
  Is supposed to be mad."

                              "I may be mad."

"You look so, sitting out here in the rain
  Studying genealogy with me
  You never saw before. What will we come to
  With all this pride of ancestry, we Yankees?
  I think we're all mad. Tell me why we're here
  Drawn into town about this cellar hole
  Like wild geese on a lake before a storm?
  What do we see in such a hole, I wonder."

"The Indians had a myth of Chicamoztoc,[41]
  Which means The Seven Caves that We Came out of.
  This is the pit from which we Starks were digged."

"You must be learned. That's what you see in it?"

"And what do you see?"

                        "Yes, what *do* I see?
  First let me look. I see raspberry vines——"

"Oh, if you're going to use your eyes, just hear
What *I* see. It's a little, little boy,
As pale and dim as a match flame in the sun;
He's groping in the cellar after jam,
He thinks it's dark and it's flooded with daylight."

"He's nothing. Listen. When I lean like this
I can make out old Grandsir Stark distinctly,—
With his pipe in his mouth and his brown jug—
Bless you, it isn't Grandsir Stark, it's Granny,
But the pipe's there and smoking and the jug.
She's after cider, the old girl, she's thirsty;
Here's hoping she gets her drink and gets out safely."

"Tell me about her. Does she look like me?"

"She should, shouldn't she, you're so many times
Over descended from her. I believe
She does look like you. Stay the way you are.
The nose is just the same, and so's the chin—
Making allowance, making due allowance."

"You poor, dear, great, great, great, great Granny!"

"See that you get her greatness right. Don't stint her."

"Yes, it's important, though you think it isn't.
I won't be teased. But see how wet I am."

"Yes, you must go; we can't stay here for ever.
But wait until I give you a hand up.
A bead of silver water more or less
Strung on your hair won't hurt your summer looks.
I wanted to try something with the noise

That the brook raises in the empty valley.
We have seen visions—now consult the voices.
Something I must have learned riding in trains
When I was young. I used the roar
To set the voices speaking out of it,
Speaking or singing, and the band-music playing.
Perhaps you have the art of what I mean.
I've never listened in among the sounds
That a brook makes in such a wild descent.
It ought to give a purer oracle."

"It's as you throw a picture on a screen:
The meaning of it all is out of you;
The voices give you what you wish to hear."

"Strangely, it's anything they wish to give."

"Then I don't know. It must be strange enough.
I wonder if it's not your make-believe.
What do you think you're like to hear to-day?"

"From the sense of our having been together—
But why take time for what I'm like to hear?
I'll tell you what the voices really say.
You will do very well right where you are
A little longer. I mustn't feel too hurried,
Or I can't give myself to hear the voices."

"Is this some trance you are withdrawing into?"

"You must be very still; you mustn't talk."

"I'll hardly breathe."

"The voices seem to say——"

"I'm waiting."

"Don't! The voices seem to say:
Call her Nausicaa, the unafraid[42]
Of an acquaintance made adventurously."

"I let you say that—on consideration."

"I don't see very well how you can help it.
You want the truth. I speak but by the voices.
You see they know I haven't had your name,
Though what a name should matter between us——"

"I shall suspect——"

"Be good. The voices say:
Call her Nausicaa, and take a timber
That you shall find lies in the cellar charred
Among the raspberries, and hew and shape it
For a door-sill or other corner piece
In a new cottage on the ancient spot.
The life is not yet all gone out of it.
And come and make your summer dwelling here,
And perhaps she will come, still unafraid,
And sit before you in the open door
With flowers in her lap until they fade,
But not come in across the sacred sill——"

"I wonder where your oracle is tending.
You can see that there's something wrong with it,
Or it would speak in dialect. Whose voice
Does it purport to speak in? Not old Grandsir's

Nor Granny's, surely. Call up one of them.
They have best right to be heard in this place."

"You seem so partial to our great-grandmother
(Nine times removed. Correct me if I err.)
You will be likely to regard as sacred
Anything she may say. But let me warn you,
Folks in her day were given to plain speaking.
You think you'd best tempt her at such a time?"

"It rests with us always to cut her off."

"Well then, it's Granny speaking: 'I dunnow!
Mebbe I'm wrong to take it as I do.
There ain't no names quite like the old ones though,
Nor never will be to my way of thinking.
One mustn't bear too hard on the new comers,
But there's a dite too many of them for comfort.[43]
I should feel easier if I could see
More of the salt wherewith they're to be salted.[44]
Son, you do as you're told! You take the timber—
It's as sound as the day when it was cut—
And begin over——' There, she'd better stop.
You can see what is troubling Granny, though.
But don't you think we sometimes make too much
Of the old stock? What counts is the ideals,
And those will bear some keeping still about."

"I can see we are going to be good friends."

"I like your 'going to be.' You said just now
It's going to rain."

"I know, and it was raining.
I let you say all that. But I must go now."

"You let me say it? on consideration?
How shall we say good-bye in such a case?"

"How shall we?"

      "Will you leave the way to me?"

"No, I don't trust your eyes. You've said enough.
Now give me your hand up.—Pick me that flower."

"Where shall we meet again?"[45]

          "Nowhere but here
Once more before we meet elsewhere."

            "In rain?"

"It ought to be in rain. Sometime in rain.
In rain to-morrow, shall we, if it rains?
But if we must, in sunshine." So she went.

THE HOUSEKEEPER

I let myself in at the kitchen door.
"It's you," she said. "I can't get up. Forgive me
Not answering your knock. I can no more
Let people in than I can keep them out.
I'm getting too old for my size, I tell them.
My fingers are about all I've the use of
So's to take any comfort. I can sew:
I help out with this beadwork that I can."

"That's a smart pair of pumps you're beading there.
Who are they for?"

       "You mean?—oh, for some miss.
I can't keep track of other people's daughters.
Lord, if I were to dream of everyone
Whose shoes I primped to dance in!"

       "And where's John?"

"Haven't you seen him? Strange what set you off
To come to his house when he's gone to yours.
You can't have passed each other. I know what:
He must have changed his mind and gone to Garlands.
He won't be long in that case. You can wait.
Though what good you can be, or anyone—
It's gone so far. You've heard? Estelle's run off."

"Yes, what's it all about? When did she go?"

"Two weeks since."

"She's in earnest, it appears."

"I'm sure she won't come back. She's hiding somewhere.
I don't know where myself. John thinks I do.
He thinks I only have to say the word,
And she'll come back. But, bless you, I'm her mother—
I can't talk to her, and, Lord, if I could!"

"It will go hard with John. What will he do?
He can't find anyone to take her place."

"Oh, if you ask me that, what *will* he do?
He gets some sort of bakeshop meals together,
With me to sit and tell him everything,
What's wanted and how much and where it is.
But when I'm gone—of course I can't stay here:
Estelle's to take me when she's settled down.
He and I only hinder one another.
I tell them they can't get me through the door, though:
I've been built in here like a big church organ.
We've been here fifteen years."

      "That's a long time
To live together and then pull apart.
How do you see him living when you're gone?
Two of you out will leave an empty house."

"I don't just see him living many years,
Left here with nothing but the furniture.
I hate to think of the old place when we're gone,
With the brook going by below the yard,
And no one here but hens blowing about.
If he could sell the place, but then, he can't:
No one will ever live on it again.

It's too run down. This is the last of it.
What I think he will do, is let things smash.
He'll sort of swear the time away. He's awful!
I never saw a man let family troubles
Make so much difference in his man's affairs.
He's just dropped everything. He's like a child.
I blame his being brought up by his mother.
He's got hay down that's been rained on three times.
He hoed a little yesterday for me:
I thought the growing things would do him good.
Something went wrong. I saw him throw the hoe
Sky-high with both hands. I can see it now—
Come here—I'll show you—in that apple tree.
That's no way for a man to do at his age:
He's fifty-five, you know, if he's a day."

"Aren't you afraid of him? What's that gun for?"

"Oh, that's been there for hawks since chicken-time.
John Hall touch me! Not if he knows his friends.
I'll say that for him, John's no threatener
Like some men folk. No one's afraid of him;
All is, he's made up his mind not to stand
What he has got to stand."

                    "Where is Estelle?
Couldn't one talk to her? What does she say?
You say you don't know where she is."

                    "Nor want to!
She thinks if it was bad to live with him,
It must be right to leave him."

                "Which is wrong!"

"Yes, but he should have married her."

"I know."

"The strain's been too much for her all these years:
I can't explain it any other way.
It's different with a man, at least with John:
He knows he's kinder than the run of men.
Better than married ought to be as good
As married—that's what he has always said.
I know the way he's felt—but all the same!"

"I wonder why he doesn't marry her
And end it."

"Too late now: she wouldn't have him.
He's given her time to think of something else.
That's his mistake. The dear knows my interest
Has been to keep the thing from breaking up.
This is a good home: I don't ask for better.
But when I've said, 'Why shouldn't they be married,'
He'd say, 'Why should they?' no more words than that."

"And after all why should they? John's been fair
I take it. What was his was always hers.
There was no quarrel about property."

"Reason enough, there was no property.
A friend or two as good as own the farm,
Such as it is. It isn't worth the mortgage."

"I mean Estelle has always held the purse."

"The rights of that are harder to get at.
I guess Estelle and I have filled the purse.
'Twas we let him have money, not he us.
John's a bad farmer. I'm not blaming him.
Take it year in, year out, he doesn't make much.
We came here for a home for me, you know,
Estelle to do the housework for the board
Of both of us. But look how it turns out:
She seems to have the housework, and besides
Half of the outdoor work, though as for that,
He'd say she does it more because she likes it.
You see our pretty things are all outdoors.
Our hens and cows and pigs are always better
Than folks like us have any business with.
Farmers around twice as well off as we
Haven't as good. They don't go with the farm.
One thing you can't help liking about John,
He's fond of nice things—too fond, some would say.
But Estelle don't complain: she's like him there.
She wants our hens to be the best there are.
You never saw this room before a show,
Full of lank, shivery, half-drowned birds
In separate coops, having their plumage done.
The smell of the wet feathers in the heat!
You spoke of John's not being safe to stay with.
You don't know what a gentle lot we are:
We wouldn't hurt a hen! You ought to see us
Moving a flock of hens from place to place.
We're not allowed to take them upside down,
All we can hold together by the legs.
Two at a time's the rule, one on each arm,
No matter how far and how many times
We have to go."

"You mean that's John's idea."

"And we live up to it; or I don't know
What childishness he wouldn't give way to.
He manages to keep the upper hand
On his own farm. He's boss. But as to hens:
We fence our flowers in and the hens range.
Nothing's too good for them. We say it pays.
John likes to tell the offers he has had,
Twenty for this cock, twenty-five for that.
He never takes the money. If they're worth
That much to sell, they're worth as much to keep.
Bless you, it's all expense, though. Reach me down
The little tin box on the cupboard shelf,
The upper shelf, the tin box. That's the one.
I'll show you. Here you are."

"What's this?"

"A bill—
For fifty dollars for one Langshang cock—[46]
Receipted. And the cock is in the yard."

"Not in a glass case, then?"

"He'd need a tall one:
He can eat off a barrel from the ground.
He's been in a glass case, as you may say.
The Crystal Palace, London. He's imported.[47]
John bought him, and we paid the bill with beads—
Wampum, I call it. Mind, we don't complain.
But you see, don't you, we take care of him."

"And like it, too. It makes it all the worse."

"It seems as if. And that's not all: he's helpless
In ways that I can hardly tell you of.
Sometimes he gets possessed to keep accounts
To see where all the money goes so fast.
You know how men will be ridiculous.
But it's just fun the way he gets bedeviled—
If he's untidy now, what will he be——?"

"It makes it all the worse. You must be blind."

"Estelle's the one. You needn't talk to me."

"Can't you and I get to the root of it?
What's the real trouble? What will satisfy her?"

"It's as I say: she's turned from him, that's all."

"But why, when she's well off? Is it the neighbours,
Being cut off from friends?"

                    "We have our friends.
That isn't it. Folks aren't afraid of us."

"She's let it worry her. You stood the strain,
And you're her mother."

                    "But I didn't always.
I didn't relish it along at first.
But I got wonted to it. And besides—
John said I was too old to have grandchildren.
But what's the use of talking when it's done?
She won't come back—it's worse than that—she can't."

"Why do you speak like that? What do you know?
What do you mean?—she's done harm to herself?"

"I mean she's married—married someone else."

"Oho, oho!"

    "You don't believe me."

                "Yes, I do,
Only too well. I knew there must be something!
So that was what was back. She's bad, that's all!"

"Bad to get married when she had the chance?"

"Nonsense! See what she's done! But who, who——"

"Who'd marry her straight out of such a mess?
Say it right out—no matter for her mother.
The man was found. I'd better name no names.
John himself won't imagine who he is."

"Then it's all up. I think I'll get away.
You'll be expecting John. I pity Estelle;
I suppose she deserves some pity, too.
You ought to have the kitchen to yourself
To break it to him. You may have the job."

"You needn't think you're going to get away.
John's almost here. I've had my eye on someone
Coming down Ryan's Hill. I thought 'twas him.
Here he is now. This box! Put it away.
And this bill."

"What's the hurry? He'll unhitch."

"No, he won't, either. He'll just drop the reins
And turn Doll out to pasture, rig and all.
She won't get far before the wheels hang up
On something—there's no harm. See, there he is!
My, but he looks as if he must have heard!"

John threw the door wide but he didn't enter.
"How are you, neighbour? Just the man I'm after.
Isn't it Hell," he said. "I want to know.
Come out here if you want to hear me talk.
I'll talk to you, old woman, afterward.
I've got some news that maybe isn't news.
What are they trying to do to me, these two?"

"Do go along with him and stop his shouting."
She raised her voice against the closing door:
"Who wants to hear your news, you—dreadful fool?"

THE FEAR

A lantern light from deeper in the barn
Shone on a man and woman in the door
And threw their lurching shadows on a house
Near by, all dark in every glossy window.
A horse's hoof pawed once the hollow floor,
And the back of the gig they stood beside
Moved in a little. The man grasped a wheel,
The woman spoke out sharply, "Whoa, stand still!"
"I saw it just as plain as a white plate,"
She said, "as the light on the dashboard ran
Along the bushes at the roadside—a man's face.
You *must* have seen it too."

                     "I didn't see it.
Are you sure——"

               "Yes, I'm sure!"

                 "—it was a face?"

"Joel, I'll have to look. I can't go in,
I can't, and leave a thing like that unsettled.
Doors locked and curtains drawn will make no difference.
I always have felt strange when we came home
To the dark house after so long an absence,
And the key rattled loudly into place
Seemed to warn someone to be getting out
At one door as we entered at another.
What if I'm right, and someone all the time—
Don't hold my arm!"

                    "I say it's someone passing."

"You speak as if this were a travelled road.
 You forget where we are. What is beyond
 That he'd be going to or coming from
 At such an hour of night, and on foot too.
 What was he standing still for in the bushes?"

"It's not so very late—it's only dark.
 There's more in it than you're inclined to say.
 Did he look like——?"

                    "He looked like anyone.
 I'll never rest to-night unless I know.
 Give me the lantern."

                    "You don't want the lantern."

She pushed past him and got it for herself.

"You're not to come," she said. "This is my business.
 If the time's come to face it, I'm the one
 To put it the right way. He'd never dare—
 Listen! He kicked a stone. Hear that, hear that!
 He's coming towards us. Joel, *go* in—please.
 Hark!—I don't hear him now. But please go in."

"In the first place you can't make me believe it's——"

"It is—or someone else he's sent to watch.
 And now's the time to have it out with him
 While we know definitely where he is.
 Let him get off and he'll be everywhere
 Around us, looking out of trees and bushes

Till I sha'n't dare to set a foot outdoors.
And I can't stand it. Joel, let me go!"

"But it's nonsense to think he'd care enough."

"You mean you couldn't understand his caring.
Oh, but you see he hadn't had enough—
Joel, I won't—I won't—I promise you.
We mustn't say hard things. You mustn't either."

"I'll be the one, if anybody goes!
But you give him the advantage with this light.
What couldn't he do to us standing here!
And if to see was what he wanted, why
He has seen all there was to see and gone."

He appeared to forget to keep his hold,
But advanced with her as she crossed the grass.

"What do you want?" she cried to all the dark.
She stretched up tall to overlook the light
That hung in both hands hot against her skirt.

"There's no one; so you're wrong," he said.

                              "There is.—
What do you want?" she cried, and then herself
Was startled when an answer really came.

"Nothing." It came from well along the road.

She reached a hand to Joel for support:
The smell of scorching woollen made her faint.
"What are you doing round this house at night?"

"Nothing." A pause: there seemed no more to say.

And then the voice again: "You seem afraid.
I saw by the way you whipped up the horse.
I'll just come forward in the lantern light
And let you see."

        "Yes, do.—Joel, go back!"

She stood her ground against the noisy steps
That came on, but her body rocked a little.

"You see," the voice said.

        "Oh," She looked and looked.

"You don't see—I've a child here by the hand."

"What's a child doing at this time of night——?"

"Out walking. Every child should have the memory
Of at least one long-after-bedtime walk.
What, son?"

        "Then I should think you'd try to find
Somewhere to walk——"

        "The highway as it happens—
We're stopping for the fortnight down at Dean's."

"But if that's all—Joel—you realize—
You won't think anything. You understand?
You understand that we have to be careful.
This is a very, very lonely place.
Joel!" She spoke as if she couldn't turn.
The swinging lantern lengthened to the ground,
It touched, it struck, it clattered and went out.

THE SELF-SEEKER

"Willis, I didn't want you here to-day:
The lawyer's coming for the company.
I'm going to sell my soul, or, rather, feet.
Five hundred dollars for the pair, you know."

"With you the feet have nearly been the soul;
And if you're going to sell them to the devil,
I want to see you do it. When's he coming?"

"I half suspect you knew, and came on purpose
To try to help me drive a better bargain."

"Well, if it's true! Yours are no common feet.
The lawyer don't know what it is he's buying:
So many miles you might have walked you won't walk.
You haven't run your forty orchids down.
What does he think?—How *are* the blessed feet?
The doctor's sure you're going to walk again?"

"He thinks I'll hobble. It's both legs and feet."

"They must be terrible—I mean to look at."

"I haven't dared to look at them uncovered.
Through the bed blankets I remind myself
Of a starfish laid out with rigid points."

"The wonder is it hadn't been your head."

"It's hard to tell you how I managed it.
When I saw the shaft had me by the coat,
I didn't try too long to pull away,
Or fumble for my knife to cut away,
I just embraced the shaft and rode it out—
Till Weiss shut off the water in the wheel-pit.
That's how I think I didn't lose my head.
But my legs got their knocks against the ceiling."

"Awful. Why didn't they throw off the belt
Instead of going clear down in the wheel-pit?"

"They say some time was wasted on the belt—
Old streak of leather—doesn't love me much
Because I make him spit fire at my knuckles,
The way Ben Franklin used to make the kite-string.
That must be it. Some days he won't stay on.
That day a woman couldn't coax him off.
He's on his rounds now with his tail in his mouth
Snatched right and left across the silver pulleys.
Everything goes the same without me there.
You can hear the small buzz saws whine, the big saw
Caterwaul to the hills around the village
As they both bite the wood. It's all our music.
One ought as a good villager to like it.
No doubt it has a sort of prosperous sound,
And it's our life."

                    "Yes, when it's not our death."

"You make that sound as if it wasn't so
With everything. What we live by we die by.
I wonder where my lawyer is. His train's in.
I want this over with; I'm hot and tired."

"You're getting ready to do something foolish."

"Watch for him, will you, Will? You let him in.
  I'd rather Mrs. Corbin didn't know;
  I've boarded here so long, she thinks she owns me.
  You're bad enough to manage without her."

"And I'm going to be worse instead of better.
  You've got to tell me how far this is gone:
  Have you agreed to any price?"

                              "Five hundred.
  Five hundred—five—five! One, two, three, four, five.
  You needn't look at me."

                    "I don't believe you."

"I told you, Willis, when you first came in.
  Don't you be hard on me. I have to take
  What I can get. You see they have the feet,
  Which gives them the advantage in the trade.
  I can't get back the feet in any case."

"But your flowers, man, you're selling out your flowers."

"Yes, that's one way to put it—all the flowers
  Of every kind everywhere in this region
  For the next forty summers—call it forty.
  But I'm not selling those, I'm giving them,
  They never earned me so much as one cent:
  Money can't pay me for the loss of them.
  No, the five hundred was the sum they named
  To pay the doctor's bill and tide me over.
  It's that or fight, and I don't want to fight—

I just want to get settled in my life,
Such as it's going to be, and know the worst,
Or best—it may not be so bad. The firm
Promise me all the shooks I want to nail."[48]

"But what about your flora of the valley?"

"You have me there. But that—you didn't think
That was worth money to me? Still I own
It goes against me not to finish it
For the friends it might bring me. By the way,
I had a letter from Burroughs—did I tell you?—[49]
About my *Cypripedium reginae*;[50]
He says it's not reported so far north.
There! there's the bell. He's rung. But you go down
And bring him up, and don't let Mrs. Corbin.—
Oh, well, we'll soon be through with it. I'm tired."

Willis brought up besides the Boston lawyer
A little barefoot girl who in the noise
Of heavy footsteps in the old frame house,
And baritone importance of the lawyer,
Stood for a while unnoticed with her hands
Shyly behind her.

      "Well, and how is Mister——"

The lawyer was already in his satchel
As if for papers that might bear the name
He hadn't at command. "You must excuse me,
I dropped in at the mill and was detained."

"Looking round, I suppose," said Willis.

"Yes,

Well, yes."

    "Hear anything that might prove useful?"

The Broken One saw Anne. "Why, here is Anne.
What do you want, dear? Come, stand by the bed;
Tell me what is it?" Anne just wagged her dress
With both hands held behind her. "Guess," she said.

"Oh, guess which hand? My, my! Once on a time
I knew a lovely way to tell for certain
By looking in the ears. But I forget it.
Er, let me see. I think I'll take the right.
That's sure to be right even if it's wrong.
Come, hold it out. Don't change.—A Ram's Horn orchid!
A Ram's Horn! What would I have got, I wonder,
If I had chosen left. Hold out the left.
Another Ram's Horn! Where did you find those,
Under what beech tree, on what woodchuck's knoll?"

Anne looked at the large lawyer at her side,
And thought she wouldn't venture on so much.

"Were there no others?"

         "There were four or five.
I knew you wouldn't let me pick them all."

"I wouldn't—so I wouldn't. You're the girl!
You see Anne has her lesson learned by heart."

"I wanted there should be some there next year."

"Of course you did. You left the rest for seed,
And for the backwoods woodchuck. You're the girl!
A Ram's Horn orchid seedpod for a woodchuck
Sounds something like. Better than farmer's beans
To a discriminating appetite,
Though the Ram's Horn is seldom to be had
In bushel lots—doesn't come on the market.
But, Anne, I'm troubled; have you told me all?
You're hiding something. That's as bad as lying.
You ask this lawyer man. And it's not safe
With a lawyer at hand to find you out.
Nothing is hidden from some people, Anne.
You don't tell me that where you found a Ram's Horn
You didn't find a Yellow Lady's Slipper.
What did I tell you? What? I'd blush, I would.
Don't you defend yourself. If it was there,
Where is it now, the Yellow Lady's Slipper?"

"Well, wait—it's common—it's too *common*."

                              "Common?
The Purple Lady's Slipper's commoner."

"I didn't bring a Purple Lady's Slipper
To *You*—to you I mean—they're both too common."

The lawyer gave a laugh among his papers
As if with some idea that she had scored.

"I've broken Anne of gathering bouquets.
It's not fair to the child. It can't be helped though:
Pressed into service means pressed out of shape.
Somehow I'll make it right with her—she'll see.
She's going to do my scouting in the field,

Over stone walls and all along a wood
And by a river bank for water flowers,
The floating Heart, with small leaf like a heart,
And at the *sinus* under water a fist[51]
Of little fingers all kept down but one,
And that thrust up to blossom in the sun
As if to say, 'You! You're the Heart's desire.'
Anne has a way with flowers to take the place
Of that she's lost: she goes down on one knee
And lifts their faces by the chin to hers
And says their names, and leaves them where they are."

The lawyer wore a watch the case of which
Was cunningly devised to make a noise
Like a small pistol when he snapped it shut
At such a time as this. He snapped it now.

"Well, Anne, go, dearie. Our affair will wait.
The lawyer man is thinking of his train.
He wants to give me lots and lots of money
Before he goes, because I hurt myself,
And it may take him I don't know how long.
But put our flowers in water first. Will, help her:
The pitcher's too full for her. There's no cup?
Just hook them on the inside of the pitcher.
Now run.—Get out your documents! You see
I have to keep on the good side of Anne.
I'm a great boy to think of number one.
And you can't blame me in the place I'm in.
Who will take care of my necessities
Unless I do?"

"A pretty interlude,"
The lawyer said. "I'm sorry, but my train—
Luckily terms are all agreed upon.
You only have to sign your name. Right—there."

"You, Will, stop making faces. Come round here
Where you can't make them. What is it you want?
I'll put you out with Anne. Be good or go."

"You don't mean you will sign that thing unread?"

"Make yourself useful then, and read it for me.
Isn't it something I have seen before?"

"You'll find it is. Let your friend look at it."

"Yes, but all that takes time, and I'm as much
In haste to get it over with as you.
But read it, read it. That's right, draw the curtain:
Half the time I don't know what's troubling me.—
What do you say, Will? Don't you be a fool,
You! crumpling folks's legal documents.
Out with it if you've any real objection."

"Five hundred dollars!"

               "What would you think right?"

"A thousand wouldn't be a cent too much;
You know it, Mr. Lawyer. The sin is
Accepting anything before he knows
Whether he's ever going to walk again.
It smells to me like a dishonest trick."

"I think—I think—from what I heard today—
   And saw myself—he would be ill-advised——"

"What did you hear, for instance?" Willis said.

"Now the place where the accident occurred——"

   The Broken One was twisted in his bed.
"This is between you two apparently.
   Where I come in is what I want to know.
   You stand up to it like a pair of cocks.
   Go outdoors if you want to fight. Spare me.
   When you come back, I'll have the papers signed.
   Will pencil do? Then, please, your fountain pen.
   One of you hold my head up from the pillow."

   Willis flung off the bed. "I wash my hands—⁵²
   I'm no match—no, and don't pretend to be——"

   The lawyer gravely capped his fountain pen.
"You're doing the wise thing: you won't regret it.
   We're very sorry for you."

                         Willis sneered:
"Who's *we?*—some stockholders in Boston?
   I'll go outdoors, by gad, and won't come back."

"Willis, bring Anne back with you when you come.
   Yes. Thanks for caring. Don't mind Will: he's savage.
   He thinks you ought to pay me for my flowers.
   You don't know what I mean about the flowers.
   Don't stop to try to now. You'll miss your train.
   Good-bye." He flung his arms around his face.

THE WOOD-PILE

Out walking in the frozen swamp one gray day
I paused and said, "I will turn back from here.
No, I will go on farther—and we shall see."
The hard snow held me, save where now and then
One foot went down. The view was all in lines
Straight up and down of tall slim trees
Too much alike to mark or name a place by
So as to say for certain I was here
Or somewhere else: I was just far from home.
A small bird flew before me. He was careful
To put a tree between us when he lighted,
And say no word to tell me who he was
Who was so foolish as to think what *he* thought.
He thought that I was after him for a feather—
The white one in his tail: like one who takes
Everything said as personal to himself.
One flight out sideways would have undeceived him.
And then there was a pile of wood for which
I forgot him and let his little fear
Carry him off the way I might have gone,
Without so much as wishing him good-night.
He went behind it to make his last stand.
It was a cord of maple, cut and split
And piled—and measured, four by four by eight.
And not another like it could I see.
No runner tracks in this year's snow looped near it.
And it was older sure than this year's cutting,
Or even last year's or the year's before.
The wood was gray and the bark warping off it

And the pile somewhat sunken. Clematis[53]
Had wound strings round and round it like a bundle.
What held it though on one side was a tree
Still growing, and on one a stake and prop,
These latter about to fall. I thought that only
Someone who lived in turning to fresh tasks
Could so forget his handiwork on which
He spent himself, the labour of his axe,
And leave it there far from a useful fireplace
To warm the frozen swamp as best it could
With the slow smokeless burning of decay.

GOOD HOURS

I had for my winter evening walk—
No one at all with whom to talk,
But I had the cottages in a row
Up to their shining eyes in snow.

And I thought I had the folk within:
I had the sound of a violin;
I had a glimpse through curtain laces
Of youthful forms and youthful faces.

I had such company outward bound.
I went till there were no cottages found.
I turned and repented, but coming back
I saw no window but that was black.

Over the snow my creaking feet
Disturbed the slumbering village street
Like profanation, by your leave,[54]
At ten o'clock of a winter eve.

MOUNTAIN INTERVAL

TO YOU

WHO LEAST NEED REMINDING

*that before this interval of the South Branch
under black mountains, there was another
interval, the Upper at Plymouth, where we
walked in spring beyond the covered bridge;
but that the first interval of all was the old
farm, our brook interval, so called by the
man we had it from in sale.*

THE ROAD NOT TAKEN

Two roads diverged in a yellow wood,
And sorry I could not travel both
And be one traveler, long I stood
And looked down one as far as I could
To where it bent in the undergrowth;

Then took the other, as just as fair,
And having perhaps the better claim,
Because it was grassy and wanted wear;
Though as for that the passing there
Had worn them really about the same,

And both that morning equally lay
In leaves no step had trodden black.
Oh, I kept the first for another day!
Yet knowing how way leads on to way,
I doubted if I should ever come back.

I shall be telling this with a sigh
Somewhere ages and ages hence:
Two roads diverged in a wood, and I—
I took the one less traveled by,
And that has made all the difference.

CHRISTMAS TREES
(A CHRISTMAS CIRCULAR LETTER)

The city had withdrawn into itself
And left at last the country to the country;
When between whirls of snow not come to lie
And whirls of foliage not yet laid, there drove
A stranger to our yard, who looked the city,
Yet did in country fashion in that there
He sat and waited till he drew us out
A-buttoning coats to ask him who he was.
He proved to be the city come again
To look for something it had left behind
And could not do without and keep its Christmas.
He asked if I would sell my Christmas trees;
My woods—the young fir balsams like a place
Where houses all are churches and have spires.
I hadn't thought of them as Christmas Trees.
I doubt if I was tempted for a moment
To sell them off their feet to go in cars
And leave the slope behind the house all bare,
Where the sun shines now no warmer than the moon.
I'd hate to have them know it if I was.
Yet more I'd hate to hold my trees except
As others hold theirs or refuse for them,
Beyond the time of profitable growth,
The trial by market everything must come to.
I dallied so much with the thought of selling.
Then whether from mistaken courtesy
And fear of seeming short of speech, or whether
From hope of hearing good of what was mine,
I said, "There aren't enough to be worth while."

"I could soon tell how many they would cut,
You let me look them over."

                               "You could look.
But don't expect I'm going to let you have them."
Pasture they spring in, some in clumps too close
That lop each other of boughs, but not a few
Quite solitary and having equal boughs
All round and round. The latter he nodded "Yes" to,
Or paused to say beneath some lovelier one,
With a buyer's moderation, "That would do."
I thought so too, but wasn't there to say so.
We climbed the pasture on the south, crossed over,
And came down on the north.

                            He said, "A thousand."

"A thousand Christmas trees!—at what apiece?"

He felt some need of softening that to me:
"A thousand trees would come to thirty dollars."

Then I was certain I had never meant
To let him have them. Never show surprise!
But thirty dollars seemed so small beside
The extent of pasture I should strip, three cents
(For that was all they figured out apiece),
Three cents so small beside the dollar friends
I should be writing to within the hour
Would pay in cities for good trees like those,
Regular vestry-trees whole Sunday Schools
Could hang enough on to pick off enough.
A thousand Christmas trees I didn't know I had!
Worth three cents more to give away than sell,

As may be shown by a simple calculation.
Too bad I couldn't lay one in a letter.
I can't help wishing I could send you one,
In wishing you herewith a Merry Christmas.

AN OLD MAN'S WINTER NIGHT[55]

All out of doors looked darkly in at him
Through the thin frost, almost in separate stars,
That gathers on the pane in empty rooms.
What kept his eyes from giving back the gaze
Was the lamp tilted near them in his hand.
What kept him from remembering what it was
That brought him to that creaking room was age.
He stood with barrels round him—at a loss.
And having scared the cellar under him
In clomping there, he scared it once again
In clomping off;—and scared the outer night,
Which has its sounds, familiar, like the roar
Of trees and crack of branches, common things,
But nothing so like beating on a box.
A light he was to no one but himself
Where now he sat, concerned with he knew what,
A quiet light, and then not even that.
He consigned to the moon, such as she was,
So late-arising, to the broken moon
As better than the sun in any case
For such a charge, his snow upon the roof,
His icicles along the wall to keep;[56]
And slept. The log that shifted with a jolt
Once in the stove, disturbed him and he shifted,
And eased his heavy breathing, but still slept.
One aged man—one man—can't fill a house,
A farm, a countryside, or if he can,
It's thus he does it of a winter night.

A PATCH OF OLD SNOW

There's a patch of old snow in a corner
   That I should have guessed
Was a blow-away paper the rain
   Had brought to rest.

It is speckled with grime as if
   Small print overspread it,
The news of a day I've forgotten—
   If I ever read it.

IN THE HOME STRETCH

She stood against the kitchen sink, and looked
Over the sink out through a dusty window
At weeds the water from the sink made tall.
She wore her cape; her hat was in her hand.
Behind her was confusion in the room,
Of chairs turned upside down to sit like people
In other chairs, and something, come to look,
For every room a house has—parlor, bed-room,
And dining-room—thrown pell-mell in the kitchen.
And now and then a smudged, infernal face
Looked in a door behind her and addressed
Her back. She always answered without turning.

"Where will I put this walnut bureau, lady?"
"Put it on top of something that's on top
    Of something else," she laughed. "Oh, put it where
    You can to-night, and go. It's almost dark;
    You must be getting started back to town."
    Another blackened face thrust in and looked
    And smiled, and when she did not turn, spoke gently,
"What are you seeing out the window, *lady?*"

"Never was I beladied so before.
    Would evidence of having been called lady
    More than so many times make me a lady
    In common law, I wonder."

                                "But I ask,
    What are you seeing out the window, lady?"

"What I'll be seeing more of in the years
  To come as here I stand and go the round
  Of many plates with towels many times."

"And what is that? You only put me off."

"Rank weeds that love the water from the dish-pan
  More than some women like the dish-pan, Joe;
  A little stretch of mowing-field for you;
  Not much of that until I come to woods
  That end all. And it's scarce enough to call
  A view."

            "And yet you think you like it, dear?"

"That's what you're so concerned to know! You hope
  I like it. Bang goes something big away
  Off there upstairs. The very tread of men
  As great as those is shattering to the frame
  Of such a little house. Once left alone,
  You and I, dear, will go with softer steps
  Up and down stairs and through the rooms, and none
  But sudden winds that snatch them from our hands
  Will ever slam the doors."

                    "I think you see
More than you like to own to out that window."

"No; for besides the things I tell you of,
  I only see the years. They come and go
  In alternation with the weeds, the field,
  The wood."

        "What kind of years?"

                             "Why, latter years—
Different from early years."

                                   "I see them, too.
You didn't count them?"

                                   "No, the further off
So ran together that I didn't try to.
It can scarce be that they would be in number
We'd care to know, for we are not young now.
And bang goes something else away off there.
It sounds as if it were the men went down,
And every crash meant one less to return
To lighted city streets we, too, have known,
But now are giving up for country darkness."

"Come from that window where you see too much for me,
And take a livelier view of things from here.
They're going. Watch this husky swarming up
Over the wheel into the sky-high seat,
Lighting his pipe now, squinting down his nose
At the flame burning downward as he sucks it."

"See how it makes his nose-side bright, a proof
How dark it's getting. Can you tell what time
It is by that? Or by the moon? The new moon!
What shoulder did I see her over? Neither.
A wire she is of silver, as new as we
To everything. Her light won't last us long.
It's something, though, to know we're going to have her
Night after night and stronger every night
To see us through our first two weeks. But, Joe,
The stove! Before they go! Knock on the window;
Ask them to help you get it on its feet.
We stand here dreaming. Hurry! Call them back!"

"They're not gone yet."

                        "We've got to have the stove,
Whatever else we want for. And a light.
Have we a piece of candle if the lamp
And oil are buried out of reach?"

                                   Again
The house was full of tramping, and the dark,
Door-filling men burst in and seized the stove.
A cannon-mouth-like hole was in the wall,
To which they set it true by eye; and then
Came up the jointed stovepipe in their hands,
So much too light and airy for their strength
It almost seemed to come ballooning up,
Slipping from clumsy clutches toward the ceiling.
"A fit!" said one, and banged a stovepipe shoulder.
"It's good luck when you move in to begin
With good luck with your stovepipe. Never mind,
It's not so bad in the country, settled down,
When people're getting on in life. You'll like it."
Joe said: "You big boys ought to find a farm,
And make good farmers, and leave other fellows
The city work to do. There's not enough
For everybody as it is in there."
"God!" one said wildly, and, when no one spoke:
"Say that to Jimmy here. He needs a farm."
But Jimmy only made his jaw recede
Fool-like, and rolled his eyes as if to say
He saw himself a farmer. Then there was a French boy
Who said with seriousness that made them laugh,
"Ma friend, you ain't know what it is you're ask."
He doffed his cap and held it with both hands
Across his chest to make as 'twere a bow:

"We're giving you our chances on de farm."
And then they all turned to with deafening boots
And put each other bodily out of the house.
"Goodby to them! We puzzle them. They think—
I don't know what they think we see in what
They leave us to: that pasture slope that seems
The back some farm presents us; and your woods
To northward from your window at the sink,
Waiting to steal a step on us whenever
We drop our eyes or turn to other things,
As in the game 'Ten-step' the children play."

"Good boys they seemed, and let them love the city.
All they could say was 'God!' when you proposed
Their coming out and making useful farmers."

"Did they make something lonesome go through you?
It would take more than them to sicken you—
Us of our bargain. But they left us so
As to our fate, like fools past reasoning with.
They almost shook *me*."

                    "It's all so much
What we have always wanted, I confess
It's seeming bad for a moment makes it seem
Even worse still, and so on down, down, down.
It's nothing; it's their leaving us at dusk.
I never bore it well when people went.
The first night after guests have gone, the house
Seems haunted or exposed. I always take
A personal interest in the locking up
At bedtime; but the strangeness soon wears off."
He fetched a dingy lantern from behind
A door. "There's that we didn't lose! And these!"—

Some matches he unpocketed. "For food—
The meals we've had no one can take from us.
I wish that everything on earth were just
As certain as the meals we've had. I wish
The meals we haven't had were, anyway.
What have you you know where to lay your hands on?"

"The bread we bought in passing at the store.
There's butter somewhere, too."

                              "Let's rend the bread.
I'll light the fire for company for you;
You'll not have any other company
Till Ed begins to get out on a Sunday
To look us over and give us his idea
Of what wants pruning, shingling, breaking up.
He'll know what he would do if he were we,
And all at once. He'll plan for us and plan
To help us, but he'll take it out in planning.
Well, you can set the table with the loaf.
Let's see you find your loaf. I'll light the fire.
I like chairs occupying other chairs
Not offering a lady—"

                              "There again, Joe!
You're tired."

                              "I'm drunk-nonsensical tired out;
Don't mind a word I say. It's a day's work
To empty one house of all household goods
And fill another with 'em fifteen miles away,
Although you do no more than dump them down."

"Dumped down in paradise we are and happy."

"It's all so much what I have always wanted,
   I can't believe it's what you wanted, too."

"Shouldn't you like to know?"

                              "I'd like to know
   If it is what you wanted, then how much
   You wanted it for me."

                         "A troubled conscience!
   You don't want me to tell if *I* don't know."

"I don't want to find out what can't be known.
   But who first said the word to come?"

                              "My dear,
   It's who first thought the thought. You're searching, Joe,
   For things that don't exist; I mean beginnings.
   Ends and beginnings—there are no such things.
   There are only middles."

                    "What is this?"
                              "This life?
   Our sitting here by lantern-light together
   Amid the wreckage of a former home?
   You won't deny the lantern isn't new.
   The stove is not, and you are not to me,
   Nor I to you."

                         "Perhaps you never were?"

"It would take me forever to recite
   All that's not new in where we find ourselves.
   New is a word for fools in towns who think

Style upon style in dress and thought at last
Must get somewhere. I've heard you say as much.
No, this is no beginning."

                              "Then an end?"

"End is a gloomy word."

                                        "Is it too late
To drag you out for just a good-night call
On the old peach trees on the knoll to grope
By starlight in the grass for a last peach
The neighbors may not have taken as their right
When the house wasn't lived in? I've been looking:
I doubt if they have left us many grapes.
Before we set ourselves to right the house,
The first thing in the morning, out we go
To go the round of apple, cherry, peach,
Pine, alder, pasture, mowing, well, and brook.
All of a farm it is."

                                    "I know this much:
I'm going to put you in your bed, if first
I have to make you build it. Come, the light."

When there was no more lantern in the kitchen,
The fire got out through crannies in the stove
And danced in yellow wrigglers on the ceiling,
As much at home as if they'd always danced there.

THE TELEPHONE

"When I was just as far as I could walk
  From here to-day,
  There was an hour
  All still
  When leaning with my head against a flower
  I heard you talk.
  Don't say I didn't, for I heard you say—
  You spoke from that flower on the window sill—
  Do you remember what it was you said?"

"First tell me what it was you thought you heard."

"Having found the flower and driven a bee away,
  I leaned my head,
  And holding by the stalk,
  I listened and I thought I caught the word—
  What was it? Did you call me by my name?
  Or did you say—
  Someone said 'Come'—I heard it as I bowed."

"I may have thought as much, but not aloud."

"Well, so I came."

MEETING AND PASSING

As I went down the hill along the wall
There was a gate I had leaned at for the view
And had just turned from when I first saw you
As you came up the hill. We met. But all
We did that day was mingle great and small
Footprints in summer dust as if we drew
The figure of our being less than two
But more than one as yet. Your parasol

Pointed the decimal off with one deep thrust.
And all the time we talked you seemed to see
Something down there to smile at in the dust.
(Oh, it was without prejudice to me!)
Afterward I went past what you had passed
Before we met and you what I had passed.

HYLA BROOK[57]

By June our brook's run out of song and speed.
Sought for much after that, it will be found
Either to have gone groping underground
(And taken with it all the Hyla breed
That shouted in the mist a month ago,
Like ghost of sleigh-bells in a ghost of snow)—
Or flourished and come up in jewel-weed,
Weak foliage that is blown upon and bent
Even against the way its waters went.
Its bed is left a faded paper sheet
Of dead leaves stuck together by the heat—
A brook to none but who remember long.
This as it will be seen is other far
Than with brooks taken otherwhere in song.
We love the things we love for what they are.

THE OVEN BIRD

There is a singer everyone has heard,
Loud, a mid-summer and a mid-wood bird,
Who makes the solid tree trunks sound again.
He says that leaves are old and that for flowers
Mid-summer is to spring as one to ten.
He says the early petal-fall is past
When pear and cherry bloom went down in showers
On sunny days a moment overcast;
And comes that other fall we name the fall.
He says the highway dust is over all.
The bird would cease and be as other birds[58]
But that he knows in singing not to sing.
The question that he frames in all but words
Is what to make of a diminished thing.

BOND AND FREE

Love has earth to which she clings
With hills and circling arms about—
Wall within wall to shut fear out.
But Thought has need of no such things,
For Thought has a pair of dauntless wings.

On snow and sand and turf, I see
Where Love has left a printed trace
With straining in the world's embrace.
And such is Love and glad to be.
But Thought has shaken his ankles free.

Thought cleaves the interstellar gloom
And sits in Sirius' disc all night,[59]
Till day makes him retrace his flight,
With smell of burning on every plume,
Back past the sun to an earthly room.

His gains in heaven are what they are.
Yet some say Love by being thrall
And simply staying possesses all
In several beauty that Thought fares far
To find fused in another star.

BIRCHES

When I see birches bend to left and right
Across the lines of straighter darker trees,
I like to think some boy's been swinging them.
But swinging doesn't bend them down to stay.
Ice-storms do that. Often you must have seen them
Loaded with ice a sunny winter morning
After a rain. They click upon themselves
As the breeze rises, and turn many-colored
As the stir cracks and crazes their enamel.
Soon the sun's warmth makes them shed crystal shells
Shattering and avalanching on the snow-crust—
Such heaps of broken glass to sweep away
You'd think the inner dome of heaven had fallen.[60]
They are dragged to the withered bracken by the load,[61]
And they seem not to break; though once they are bowed
So low for long, they never right themselves:
You may see their trunks arching in the woods
Years afterwards, trailing their leaves on the ground
Like girls on hands and knees that throw their hair
Before them over their heads to dry in the sun.
But I was going to say when Truth broke in
With all her matter-of-fact about the ice-storm
(Now am I free to be poetical?)
I should prefer to have some boy bend them
As he went out and in to fetch the cows—
Some boy too far from town to learn baseball,
Whose only play was what he found himself,
Summer or winter, and could play alone.
One by one he subdued his father's trees

By riding them down over and over again
Until he took the stiffness out of them,
And not one but hung limp, not one was left
For him to conquer. He learned all there was
To learn about not launching out too soon
And so not carrying the tree away
Clear to the ground. He always kept his poise
To the top branches, climbing carefully
With the same pains you use to fill a cup
Up to the brim, and even above the brim.
Then he flung outward, feet first, with a swish,
Kicking his way down through the air to the ground.
So was I once myself a swinger of birches.
And so I dream of going back to be.
It's when I'm weary of considerations,
And life is too much like a pathless wood
Where your face burns and tickles with the cobwebs
Broken across it, and one eye is weeping
From a twig's having lashed across it open.
I'd like to get away from earth awhile
And then come back to it and begin over.
May no fate willfully misunderstand me
And half grant what I wish and snatch me away
Not to return. Earth's the right place for love:
I don't know where it's likely to go better.
I'd like to go by climbing a birch tree,
And climb black branches up a snow-white trunk
Toward heaven, till the tree could bear no more,
But dipped its top and set me down again.
That would be good both going and coming back.
One could do worse than be a swinger of birches.

PEA BRUSH

I walked down alone Sunday after church
   To the place where John has been cutting trees
To see for myself about the birch
   He said I could have to bush my peas.

The sun in the new-cut narrow gap
   Was hot enough for the first of May,
And stifling hot with the odor of sap
   From stumps still bleeding their life away.

The frogs that were peeping a thousand shrill
   Wherever the ground was low and wet,
The minute they heard my step went still
   To watch me and see what I came to get.

Birch boughs enough piled everywhere!—
   All fresh and sound from the recent axe.
Time someone came with cart and pair
   And got them off the wild flowers' backs.

They might be good for garden things
   To curl a little finger round,
The same as you seize cat's-cradle strings,
   And lift themselves up off the ground.

Small good to anything growing wild,
   They were crooking many a trillium[62]
That had budded before the boughs were piled
   And since it was coming up had to come.

PUTTING IN THE SEED

You come to fetch me from my work to-night
When supper's on the table, and we'll see
If I can leave off burying the white
Soft petals fallen from the apple tree.
(Soft petals, yes, but not so barren quite,
Mingled with these, smooth bean and wrinkled pea;)
And go along with you ere you lose sight
Of what you came for and become like me,
Slave to a springtime passion for the earth.
How Love burns through the Putting in the Seed
On through the watching for that early birth
When, just as the soil tarnishes with weed,
The sturdy seedling with arched body comes
Shouldering its way and shedding the earth crumbs.

A TIME TO TALK

When a friend calls to me from the road
And slows his horse to a meaning walk,
I don't stand still and look around
On all the hills I haven't hoed,
And shout from where I am, What is it?
No, not as there is a time to talk.
I thrust my hoe in the mellow ground,
Blade-end up and five feet tall,
And plod: I go up to the stone wall
For a friendly visit.

THE COW IN APPLE TIME

Something inspires the only cow of late
To make no more of a wall than an open gate,
And think no more of wall-builders than fools.
Her face is flecked with pomace and she drools[63]
A cider syrup. Having tasted fruit,
She scorns a pasture withering to the root.
She runs from tree to tree where lie and sweeten
The windfalls spiked with stubble and worm-eaten.
She leaves them bitten when she has to fly.
She bellows on a knoll against the sky.
Her udder shrivels and the milk goes dry.

AN ENCOUNTER

Once on the kind of day called "weather breeder,"
When the heat slowly hazes and the sun
By its own power seems to be undone,
I was half boring through, half climbing through
A swamp of cedar. Choked with oil of cedar
And scurf of plants, and weary and over-heated,[64]
And sorry I ever left the road I knew,
I paused and rested on a sort of hook
That had me by the coat as good as seated,
And since there was no other way to look,
Looked up toward heaven, and there against the blue,
Stood over me a resurrected tree,
A tree that had been down and raised again—
A barkless spectre. He had halted too,
As if for fear of treading upon me.
I saw the strange position of his hands—
Up at his shoulders, dragging yellow strands
Of wire with something in it from men to men.
"You here?" I said. "Where aren't you nowadays
And what's the news you carry—if you know?
And tell me where you're off for—Montreal?
Me? I'm not off for anywhere at all.
Sometimes I wander out of beaten ways
Half looking for the orchid Calypso."

RANGE-FINDING[65]

The battle rent a cobweb diamond-strung
And cut a flower beside a ground bird's nest
Before it stained a single human breast.
The stricken flower bent double and so hung.
And still the bird revisited her young.
A butterfly its fall had dispossessed
A moment sought in air his flower of rest,
Then lightly stooped to it and fluttering clung.
On the bare upland pasture there had spread
O'ernight 'twixt mullein stalks a wheel of thread[66]
And straining cables wet with silver dew.
A sudden passing bullet shook it dry.
The indwelling spider ran to greet the fly,
But finding nothing, sullenly withdrew.

THE HILL WIFE

LONELINESS
(Her Word)

One ought not to have to care
    So much as you and I
Care when the birds come round the house
    To seem to say good-bye;

Or care so much when they come back
    With whatever it is they sing;
The truth being we are as much
    Too glad for the one thing

As we are too sad for the other here—
    With birds that fill their breasts
But with each other and themselves
    And their built or driven nests.

HOUSE FEAR

Always—I tell you this they learned—
Always at night when they returned
To the lonely house from far away
To lamps unlighted and fire gone gray,
They learned to rattle the lock and key
To give whatever might chance to be
Warning and time to be off in flight:
And preferring the out- to the in-door night,

They learned to leave the house-door wide
Until they had lit the lamp inside.

THE SMILE
(Her Word)

I didn't like the way he went away.
That smile! It never came of being gay.
Still he smiled—did you see him?—I was sure!
Perhaps because we gave him only bread
And the wretch knew from that that we were poor.
Perhaps because he let us give instead
Of seizing from us as he might have seized.
Perhaps he mocked at us for being wed,
Or being very young (and he was pleased
To have a vision of us old and dead).
I wonder how far down the road he's got.
He's watching from the woods as like as not.

THE OFT-REPEATED DREAM

She had no saying dark enough
    For the dark pine that kept
Forever trying the window-latch
    Of the room where they slept.

The tireless but ineffectual hands
    That with every futile pass
Made the great tree seem as a little bird
    Before the mystery of glass!

It never had been inside the room,
  And only one of the two
Was afraid in an oft-repeated dream
  Of what the tree might do.

THE IMPULSE

It was too lonely for her there,
  And too wild,
And since there were but two of them,
  And no child,
And work was little in the house,
  She was free,
And followed where he furrowed field,
  Or felled tree.

She rested on a log and tossed
  The fresh chips,
With a song only to herself
  On her lips.
And once she went to break a bough
  Of black alder.
She strayed so far she scarcely heard
  When he called her—

And didn't answer—didn't speak—
  Or return.
She stood, and then she ran and hid
  In the fern.
He never found her, though he looked
  Everywhere,
And he asked at her mother's house
  Was she there.

Sudden and swift and light as that
    The ties gave,
And he learned of finalities
    Besides the grave.

THE BONFIRE

"Oh, let's go up the hill and scare ourselves,
As reckless as the best of them to-night,
By setting fire to all the brush we piled
With pitchy hands to wait for rain or snow.
Oh, let's not wait for rain to make it safe.
The pile is ours: we dragged it bough on bough
Down dark converging paths between the pines.
Let's not care what we do with it to-night.
Divide it? No! But burn it as one pile
The way we piled it. And let's be the talk
Of people brought to windows by a light
Thrown from somewhere against their wall-paper.
Rouse them all, both the free and not so free
With saying what they'd like to do to us
For what they'd better wait till we have done.
Let's all but bring to life this old volcano,
If that is what the mountain ever was—
And scare ourselves. Let wild fire loose we will. . . . "

"And scare you too?" the children said together.

"Why wouldn't it scare me to have a fire
Begin in smudge with ropy smoke and know
That still, if I repent, I may recall it,
But in a moment not: a little spurt
Of burning fatness, and then nothing but
The fire itself can put it out, and that
By burning out, and before it burns out
It will have roared first and mixed sparks with stars,

And sweeping round it with a flaming sword,
Made the dim trees stand back in wider circle—
Done so much and I know not how much more
I mean it shall not do if I can bind it.
Well if it doesn't with its draft bring on
A wind to blow in earnest from some quarter,
As once it did with me upon an April.
The breezes were so spent with winter blowing
They seemed to fail the bluebirds under them
Short of the perch their languid flight was toward;
And my flame made a pinnacle to heaven
As I walked once round it in possession.
But the wind out of doors—you know the saying.
There came a gust. You used to think the trees
Made wind by fanning since you never knew
It blow but that you saw the trees in motion.
Something or someone watching made that gust.
It put the flame tip-down and dabbed the grass
Of over-winter with the least tip-touch
Your tongue gives salt or sugar in your hand.
The place it reached to blackened instantly.
The black was all there was by day-light,
That and the merest curl of cigarette smoke—
And a flame slender as the hepaticas,[67]
Blood-root, and violets so soon to be now.
But the black spread like black death on the ground,
And I think the sky darkened with a cloud
Like winter and evening coming on together.
There were enough things to be thought of then.
Where the field stretches toward the north
And setting sun to Hyla brook, I gave it
To flames without twice thinking, where it verges
Upon the road, to flames too, though in fear
They might find fuel there, in withered brake,[68]

Grass its full length, old silver golden-rod,
And alder and grape vine entanglement,
To leap the dusty deadline. For my own
I took what front there was beside. I knelt
And thrust hands in and held my face away.
Fight such a fire by rubbing not by beating.
A board is the best weapon if you have it.
I had my coat. And oh, I knew, I knew,
And said out loud, I couldn't bide the smother
And heat so close in; but the thought of all
The woods and town on fire by me, and all
The town turned out to fight for me—that held me.
I trusted the brook barrier, but feared
The road would fail; and on that side the fire
Died not without a noise of crackling wood—
Of something more than tinder-grass and weed—
That brought me to my feet to hold it back
By leaning back myself, as if the reins
Were round my neck and I was at the plough.
I won! But I'm sure no one ever spread
Another color over a tenth the space
That I spread coal-black over in the time
It took me. Neighbors coming home from town
Couldn't believe that so much black had come there
While they had backs turned, that it hadn't been there
When they had passed an hour or so before
Going the other way and they not seen it.
They looked about for someone to have done it.
But there was no one. I was somewhere wondering
Where all my weariness had gone and why
I walked so light on air in heavy shoes
In spite of a scorched Fourth-of-July feeling.
Why wouldn't I be scared remembering that?"

"If it scares you, what will it do to us?"

"Scare you. But if you shrink from being scared,
What would you say to war if it should come?
That's what for reasons I should like to know—
If you can comfort me by any answer."

"Oh, but war's not for children—it's for men."

"Now we are digging almost down to China.
My dears, my dears, you thought that—we all thought it.
So your mistake was ours. Haven't you heard, though,
About the ships where war has found them out
At sea, about the towns where war has come
Through opening clouds at night with droning speed
Further o'erhead than all but stars and angels,—
And children in the ships and in the towns?
Haven't you heard what we have lived to learn?
Nothing so new—something we had forgotten:
War is for everyone, for children too.
I wasn't going to tell you and I mustn't.
The best way is to come up hill with me
And have our fire and laugh and be afraid."

A GIRL'S GARDEN

A neighbor of mine in the village
   Likes to tell how one spring
When she was a girl on the farm, she did
   A childlike thing.

One day she asked her father
   To give her a garden plot
To plant and tend and reap herself,
   And he said, "Why not?"

In casting about for a corner
   He thought of an idle bit
Of walled-off ground where a shop had stood,
   And he said, "Just it."

And he said, "That ought to make you
   An ideal one-girl farm,
And give you a chance to put some strength
   On your slim-jim arm."

It was not enough of a garden,
   Her father said, to plough;
So she had to work it all by hand,
   But she don't mind now.

She wheeled the dung in the wheelbarrow
   Along a stretch of road;
But she always ran away and left
   Her not-nice load.

And hid from anyone passing.
  And then she begged the seed.
She says she thinks she planted one
  Of all things but weed.

A hill each of potatoes,
  Radishes, lettuce, peas,
Tomatoes, beets, beans, pumpkins, corn,
  And even fruit trees.

And yes, she has long mistrusted
  That a cider apple tree
In bearing there to-day is hers,
  Or at least may be.

Her crop was a miscellany
  When all was said and done,
A little bit of everything,
  A great deal of none.

Now when she sees in the village
  How village things go,
Just when it seems to come in right,
  She says, *"I* know!

It's as when I was a farmer——"
  Oh, never by way of advice!
And she never sins by telling the tale
  To the same person twice.

THE EXPOSED NEST

You were forever finding some new play.
So when I saw you down on hands and knees
In the meadow, busy with the new-cut hay,
Trying, I thought, to set it up on end,
I went to show you how to make it stay,
If that was your idea, against the breeze,
And, if you asked me, even help pretend
To make it root again and grow afresh.
But 'twas no make-believe with you to-day,
Nor was the grass itself your real concern,
Though I found your hand full of wilted fern,
Steel-bright June-grass, and blackening heads of clover.
'Twas a nest full of young birds on the ground
The cutter-bar had just gone champing over
(Miraculously without tasting flesh)
And left defenseless to the heat and light.
You wanted to restore them to their right
Of something interposed between their sight
And too much world at once—could means be found.
The way the nest-full every time we stirred
Stood up to us as to a mother-bird
Whose coming home has been too long deferred,
Made me ask would the mother-bird return
And care for them in such a change of scene
And might our meddling make her more afraid.
That was a thing we could not wait to learn.
We saw the risk we took in doing good,
But dared not spare to do the best we could
Though harm should come of it; so built the screen

You had begun, and gave them back their shade.
All this to prove we cared. Why is there then
No more to tell? We turned to other things.
I haven't any memory—have you?—
Of ever coming to the place again
To see if the birds lived the first night through,
And so at last to learn to use their wings.

"OUT, OUT—"

The buzz-saw snarled and rattled in the yard
And made dust and dropped stove-length sticks of wood,
Sweet-scented stuff when the breeze drew across it.
And from there those that lifted eyes could count
Five mountain ranges one behind the other
Under the sunset far into Vermont.
And the saw snarled and rattled, snarled and rattled,
As it ran light, or had to bear a load.
And nothing happened: day was all but done.
Call it a day, I wish they might have said
To please the boy by giving him the half hour
That a boy counts so much when saved from work.
His sister stood beside them in her apron
To tell them "Supper." At the word, the saw,
As if to prove saws knew what supper meant,
Leaped out at the boy's hand, or seemed to leap—
He must have given the hand. However it was,
Neither refused the meeting. But the hand!
The boy's first outcry was a rueful laugh,
As he swung toward them holding up the hand
Half in appeal, but half as if to keep
The life from spilling. Then the boy saw all—
Since he was old enough to know, big boy
Doing a man's work, though a child at heart—
He saw all spoiled. "Don't let him cut my hand off—
The doctor, when he comes. Don't let him, sister!"
So. But the hand was gone already.
The doctor put him in the dark of ether.
He lay and puffed his lips out with his breath.

And then—the watcher at his pulse took fright.
No one believed. They listened at his heart.
Little—less—nothing!—and that ended it.
No more to build on there. And they, since they
Were not the one dead, turned to their affairs.

BROWN'S DESCENT
OR
THE WILLY-NILLY SLIDE

Brown lived at such a lofty farm
    That everyone for miles could see
His lantern when he did his chores
    In winter after half-past three.

And many must have seen him make
    His wild descent from there one night,
'Cross lots, 'cross walls, 'cross everything,[69]
    Describing rings of lantern light.

Between the house and barn the gale
    Got him by something he had on
And blew him out on the icy crust
    That cased the world, and he was gone!

Walls were all buried, trees were few:
    He saw no stay unless he stove
A hole in somewhere with his heel.
    But though repeatedly he strove

And stamped and said things to himself,
    And sometimes something seemed to yield,
He gained no foothold, but pursued
    His journey down from field to field.

Sometimes he came with arms outspread
    Like wings, revolving in the scene
Upon his longer axis, and
    With no small dignity of mien.

Faster or slower as he chanced,
  Sitting or standing as he chose,
According as he feared to risk
  His neck, or thought to spare his clothes,

He never let the lantern drop.
  And some exclaimed who saw afar
The figures he described with it,
  "I wonder what those signals are

Brown makes at such an hour of night!
  He's celebrating something strange.
I wonder if he's sold his farm,
  Or been made Master of the Grange."⁷⁰

He reeled, he lurched, he bobbed, he checked;
  He fell and made the lantern rattle
(But saved the light from going out.)
  So half-way down he fought the battle

Incredulous of his own bad luck.
  And then becoming reconciled
To everything, he gave it up
  And came down like a coasting child.

"Well—I—be—" that was all he said,
  As standing in the river road,
He looked back up the slippery slope
  (Two miles it was) to his abode.

Sometimes as an authority
  On motor-cars, I'm asked if I
Should say our stock was petered out,
  And this is my sincere reply:

Yankees are what they always were.
     Don't think Brown ever gave up hope
Of getting home again because
     He couldn't climb that slippery slope;

Or even thought of standing there
     Until the January thaw
Should take the polish off the crust.
     He bowed with grace to natural law,

And then went round it on his feet,
     After the manner of our stock;
Not much concerned for those to whom,
     At that particular time o'clock,

It must have looked as if the course
     He steered was really straight away
From that which he was headed for—
     Not much concerned for them, I say:

No more so than became a man—
     And politician at odd seasons.
I've kept Brown standing in the cold
     While I invested him with reasons;

But now he snapped his eyes three times;
     Then shook his lantern, saying, "Ile's
'Bout out!" and took the long way home[71]
     By road, a matter of several miles.

THE GUM-GATHERER

There overtook me and drew me in
To his down-hill, early-morning stride,
And set me five miles on my road
Better than if he had had me ride,
A man with a swinging bag for load
And half the bag wound round his hand.
We talked like barking above the din
Of water we walked along beside.
And for my telling him where I'd been
And where I lived in mountain land
To be coming home the way I was,
He told me a little about himself.
He came from higher up in the pass
Where the grist of the new-beginning brooks
Is blocks split off the mountain mass—
And hopeless grist enough it looks
Ever to grind to soil for grass.
(The way it is will do for moss.)
There he had built his stolen shack.
It had to be a stolen shack
Because of the fears of fire and loss
That trouble the sleep of lumber folk:
Visions of half the world burned black
And the sun shrunken yellow in smoke.
We know who when they come to town
Bring berries under the wagon seat,
Or a basket of eggs between their feet;
What this man brought in a cotton sack
Was gum, the gum of the mountain spruce.

He showed me lumps of the scented stuff
Like uncut jewels, dull and rough.
It comes to market golden brown;
But turns to pink between the teeth.

I told him this is a pleasant life
To set your breast to the bark of trees
That all your days are dim beneath,
And reaching up with a little knife,
To loose the resin and take it down
And bring it to market when you please.

THE LINE-GANG

Here come the line-gang pioneering by.
They throw a forest down less cut than broken.
They plant dead trees for living, and the dead
They string together with a living thread.
They string an instrument against the sky
Wherein words whether beaten out or spoken
Will run as hushed as when they were a thought.
But in no hush they string it: they go past
With shouts afar to pull the cable taut,
To hold it hard until they make it fast,
To ease away—they have it. With a laugh,
An oath of towns that set the wild at naught
They bring the telephone and telegraph.

THE VANISHING RED

He is said to have been the last Red Man
In Acton. And the Miller is said to have laughed—
If you like to call such a sound a laugh.
But he gave no one else a laugher's license.
For he turned suddenly grave as if to say,
"Whose business,—if I take it on myself,
Whose business—but why talk round the barn?—
When it's just that I hold with getting a thing done with."
You can't get back and see it as he saw it.
It's too long a story to go into now.
You'd have to have been there and lived it.
Then you wouldn't have looked on it as just a matter
Of who began it between the two races.

Some guttural exclamation of surprise
The Red Man gave in poking about the mill
Over the great big thumping shuffling mill-stone
Disgusted the Miller physically as coming
From one who had no right to be heard from.
"Come, John," he said, "you want to see the wheel pit?"

He took him down below a cramping rafter,
And showed him, through a manhole in the floor,
The water in desperate straits like frantic fish,
Salmon and sturgeon, lashing with their tails.
Then he shut down the trap door with a ring in it

That jangled even above the general noise,
And came up stairs alone—and gave that laugh,
And said something to a man with a meal-sack
That the man with the meal-sack didn't catch—then.
Oh, yes, he showed John the wheel pit all right.

SNOW

The three stood listening to a fresh access
Of wind that caught against the house a moment,
Gulped snow, and then blew free again—the Coles
Dressed, but dishevelled from some hours of sleep,
Meserve belittled in the great skin coat he wore.

Meserve was first to speak. He pointed backward
Over his shoulder with his pipe-stem, saying,
"You can just see it glancing off the roof
Making a great scroll upward toward the sky,
Long enough for recording all our names on.—
I think I'll just call up my wife and tell her
I'm here—so far—and starting on again.
I'll call her softly so that if she's wise
And gone to sleep, she needn't wake to answer."
Three times he barely stirred the bell, then listened.
"Why, Lett, still up? Lett, I'm at Cole's. I'm late.
I called you up to say Good-night from here
Before I went to say Good-morning there.—
I thought I would.—I know, but, Lett—I know—
I could, but what's the sense? The rest won't be
So bad.—Give me an hour for it.—Ho, ho,
Three hours to here! But that was all up hill;
The rest is down.—Why no, no, not a wallow:
They kept their heads and took their time to it
Like darlings, both of them. They're in the barn.—
My dear, I'm coming just the same. I didn't
Call you to ask you to invite me home.—"
He lingered for some word she wouldn't say,

Said it at last himself, "Good-night," and then,
Getting no answer, closed the telephone.
The three stood in the lamplight round the table
With lowered eyes a moment till he said,
"I'll just see how the horses are."

                                    "Yes, do,"
Both the Coles said together. Mrs. Cole
Added: "You can judge better after seeing.—
I want you here with me, Fred. Leave him here,
Brother Meserve. You know to find your way
Out through the shed."

                              "I guess I know my way,
I guess I know where I can find my name
Carved in the shed to tell me who I am
If it don't tell me where I am. I used
To play—"

                        "You tend your horses and come back.
Fred Cole, you're going to let him!"

                                    "Well, aren't you?
How can you help yourself?"

                                    "I called him Brother.
Why did I call him that?"

                                    "It's right enough.
That's all you ever heard him called round here.
He seems to have lost off his Christian name."

"Christian enough I should call that myself.
He took no notice, did he? Well, at least

I didn't use it out of love of him,
The dear knows. I detest the thought of him
With his ten children under ten years old.
I hate his wretched little Racker Sect,[72]
All's ever I heard of it, which isn't much.
But that's not saying—Look, Fred Cole, it's twelve,
Isn't it, now? He's been here half an hour.
He says he left the village store at nine.
Three hours to do four miles—a mile an hour
Or not much better. Why, it doesn't seem
As if a man could move that slow and move.
Try to think what he did with all that time.
And three miles more to go!"

                "Don't let him go.
Stick to him, Helen. Make him answer you.
That sort of man talks straight on all his life
From the last thing he said himself, stone deaf
To anything anyone else may say.
I should have thought, though, you could make him hear you."

"What is he doing out a night like this?
Why can't he stay at home?"

             "He had to preach."

"It's no night to be out."

              "He may be small,
He may be good, but one thing's sure, he's tough."

"And strong of stale tobacco."

             "He'll pull through."

"You only say so. Not another house
Or shelter to put into from this place
To theirs. I'm going to call his wife again."

"Wait and he may. Let's see what he will do.
Let's see if he will think of her again.
But then I doubt he's thinking of himself.
He doesn't look on it as anything."

"He shan't go—there!"

                                        "It *is* a night, my dear."

"One thing: he didn't drag God into it."

"He don't consider it a case for God."

"You think so, do you? You don't know the kind.
He's getting up a miracle this minute.
Privately—to himself, right now, he's thinking
He'll make a case of it if he succeeds,
But keep still if he fails."

                                "Keep still all over.
He'll be dead—dead and buried."

                                        "Such a trouble!
Not but I've every reason not to care
What happens to him if it only takes
Some of the sanctimonious conceit
Out of one of those pious scalawags."

"Nonsense to that! You want to see him safe."

"You like the runt."

                        "Don't you a little?"

                                   "Well,
I don't like what he's doing, which is what
You like, and like him for."

                         "Oh, yes you do.
You like your fun as well as anyone;
Only you women have to put these airs on
To impress men. You've got us so ashamed
Of being men we can't look at a good fight
Between two boys and not feel bound to stop it.
Let the man freeze an ear or two, I say.—
He's here. I leave him all to you. Go in
And save his life.—All right, come in, Meserve.
Sit down, sit down. How did you find the horses?"

"Fine, fine."

           "And ready for some more? My wife here
Says it won't do. You've got to give it up."

"Won't you to please me? Please! If I say please?
Mr. Meserve, I'll leave it to *your* wife.
What *did* your wife say on the telephone?"

Meserve seemed to heed nothing but the lamp
Or something not far from it on the table.
By straightening out and lifting a forefinger,
He pointed with his hand from where it lay
Like a white crumpled spider on his knee:
"That leaf there in your open book! It moved

Just then, I thought. It's stood erect like that,
There on the table, ever since I came,
Trying to turn itself backward or forward,
I've had my eye on it to make out which;
If forward, then it's with a friend's impatience—
You see I know—to get you on to things
It wants to see how you will take, if backward
It's from regret for something you have passed
And failed to see the good of. Never mind,
Things must expect to come in front of us
A many times—I don't say just how many—
That varies with the things—before we see them.
One of the lies would make it out that nothing
Ever presents itself before us twice.
Where would we be at last if that were so?
Our very life depends on everything's
Recurring till we answer from within.
The thousandth time may prove the charm.—That leaf!
It can't turn either way. It needs the wind's help.
But the wind didn't move it if it moved.
It moved itself. The wind's at naught in here.
It couldn't stir so sensitively poised
A thing as that. It couldn't reach the lamp
To get a puff of black smoke from the flame,
Or blow a rumple in the collie's coat.
You make a little foursquare block of air,
Quiet and light and warm, in spite of all
The illimitable dark and cold and storm,
And by so doing give these three, lamp, dog,
And book-leaf, that keep near you, their repose;
Though for all anyone can tell, repose
May be the thing you haven't, yet you give it.
So false it is that what we haven't we can't give;
So false, that what we always say is true.

I'll have to turn the leaf if no one else will.
It won't lie down. Then let it stand. Who cares?"

"I shouldn't want to hurry you, Meserve,
But if you're going—Say you'll stay, you know?
But let me raise this curtain on a scene,
And show you how it's piling up against you.
You see the snow-white through the white of frost?
Ask Helen how far up the sash it's climbed
Since last we read the gauge."

                              "It looks as if
Some pallid thing had squashed its features flat
And its eyes shut with overeagerness
To see what people found so interesting
In one another, and had gone to sleep
Of its own stupid lack of understanding,
Or broken its white neck of mushroom stuff
Short off, and died against the window-pane."

"Brother Meserve, take care, you'll scare yourself
More than you will us with such nightmare talk.
It's you it matters to, because it's you
Who have to go out into it alone."

"Let him talk, Helen, and perhaps he'll stay."

"Before you drop the curtain—I'm reminded:
You recollect the boy who came out here
To breathe the air one winter—had a room
Down at the Averys'? Well, one sunny morning
After a downy storm, he passed our place
And found me banking up the house with snow.
And I was burrowing in deep for warmth,

Piling it well above the window-sills.
The snow against the window caught his eye.
'Hey, that's a pretty thought'—those were his words.
'So you can think it's six feet deep outside,
While you sit warm and read up balanced rations.
You can't get too much winter in the winter.'
Those were his words. And he went home and all
But banked the daylight out of Avery's windows.
Now you and I would go to no such length.
At the same time you can't deny it makes
It not a mite worse, sitting here, we three,
Playing our fancy, to have the snowline run
So high across the pane outside. There where
There is a sort of tunnel in the frost
More like a tunnel than a hole—way down
At the far end of it you see a stir
And quiver like the frayed edge of the drift
Blown in the wind. I *like* that—I like *that*.
Well, now I leave you, people."

                                   "Come, Meserve,
We thought you were deciding not to go—
The ways you found to say the praise of comfort
And being where you are. You want to stay."

"I'll own it's cold for such a fall of snow.
This house is frozen brittle, all except
This room you sit in. If you think the wind
Sounds further off, it's not because it's dying;
You're further under in the snow—that's all—
And feel it less. Hear the soft bombs of dust
It bursts against us at the chimney mouth,
And at the eaves. I like it from inside
More than I shall out in it. But the horses

Are rested and it's time to say good-night,
And let you get to bed again. Good-night,
Sorry I had to break in on your sleep."

"Lucky for you you did. Lucky for you
You had us for a half-way station
To stop at. If you were the kind of man
Paid heed to women, you'd take my advice
And for your family's sake stay where you are.
But what good is my saying it over and over?
You've done more than you had a right to think
You could do—*now*. You know the risk you take
In going on."

          "Our snow-storms as a rule
Aren't looked on as man-killers, and although
I'd rather be the beast that sleeps the sleep
Under it all, his door sealed up and lost,
Than the man fighting it to keep above it,
Yet think of the small birds at roost and not
In nests. Shall I be counted less than they are?
Their bulk in water would be frozen rock
In no time out to-night. And yet to-morrow
They will come budding boughs from tree to tree
Flirting their wings and saying Chickadee,[73]
As if not knowing what you meant by the word storm."

"But why when no one wants you to go on?
Your wife—she doesn't want you to. We don't,
And you yourself don't want to. Who else is there?"

"Save us from being cornered by a woman.
Well, there's"—She told Fred afterward that in
The pause right there, she thought the dreaded word

Was coming, "God." But no, he only said
"Well, there's—the storm. That says I must go on.
That wants me as a war might if it came.
Ask any man."

                          He threw her that as something
To last her till he got outside the door.
He had Cole with him to the barn to see him off.
When Cole returned he found his wife still standing
Beside the table near the open book,
Not reading it.

                          "Well, what kind of a man
Do you call that?" she said.

                                    "He had the gift
Of words, or is it tongues, I ought to say?"[74]

"Was ever such a man for seeing likeness?"

"Or disregarding people's civil questions—
What? We've found out in one hour more about him
Than we had seeing him pass by in the road
A thousand times. If that's the way he preaches!
You didn't think you'd keep him after all.
Oh, I'm not blaming you. He didn't leave you
Much say in the matter, and I'm just as glad
We're not in for a night of him. No sleep
If he had stayed. The least thing set him going.
It's quiet as an empty church without him."

"But how much better off are we as it is?
We'll have to sit here till we know he's safe."

"Yes, I suppose you'll want to, but I shouldn't.
He knows what he can do, or he wouldn't try.
Get into bed I say, and get some rest.
He won't come back, and if he telephones,
It won't be for an hour or two."

                                    "Well then.
We can't be any help by sitting here
And living his fight through with him, I suppose."

                    ★   ★   ★

Cole had been telephoning in the dark.
Mrs. Cole's voice came from an inner room:
"Did she call you or you call her?"

                                    "She me.
You'd better dress: you won't go back to bed.
We must have been asleep: it's three and after."

"Had she been ringing long? I'll get my wrapper.
I want to speak to her."

                                "All she said was,
He hadn't come and had he really started."

"She knew he had, poor thing, two hours ago."

"He had the shovel. He'll have made a fight."

"Why did I ever let him leave this house!"

"Don't begin that. You did the best you could
To keep him—though perhaps you didn't quite

Conceal a wish to see him show the spunk
To disobey you. Much his wife'll thank you."

"Fred, after all I said! You shan't make out
That it was any way but what it was.
Did she let on by any word she said
She didn't thank me?"

                              "When I told her 'Gone,'
'Well then,' she said, and 'Well then'—like a threat.
And then her voice came scraping slow: 'Oh, you,
Why did you let him go?'"

                              "Asked why we let him?
You let me there. I'll ask her why she let him.
She didn't dare to speak when he was here.
Their number's—twenty-one? The thing won't work.
Someone's receiver's down. The handle stumbles.
The stubborn thing, the way it jars your arm!
It's theirs. She's dropped it from her hand and gone."

"Try speaking. Say 'Hello!'"

                              "Hello. Hello."

"What do you hear?"

                              "I hear an empty room—
You know—it sounds that way. And yes, I hear—
I think I hear a clock—and windows rattling.
No step though. If she's there she's sitting down."

"Shout, she may hear you."

"Shouting is no good."

"Keep speaking then."

"Hello. Hello. Hello.
You don't suppose—? She wouldn't go out doors?"

"I'm half afraid that's just what she might do."

"And leave the children?"

"Wait and call again.
You can't hear whether she has left the door
Wide open and the wind's blown out the lamp
And the fire's died and the room's dark and cold?"

"One of two things, either she's gone to bed
Or gone out doors."

"In which case both are lost.
Do you know what she's like? Have you ever met her?
It's strange she doesn't want to speak to us."

"Fred, see if you can hear what I hear. Come."

"A clock maybe."

"Don't you hear something else?"

"Not talking."
                    "No."

"Why, yes, I hear—what is it?"

"What do you say it is?"

        "A baby's crying!
Frantic it sounds, though muffled and far off.
Its mother wouldn't let it cry like that,
Not if she's there."

            "What do you make of it?"

"There's only one thing possible to make,
That is, assuming—that she has gone out.
Of course she hasn't though." They both sat down
Helpless. "There's nothing we can do till morning."

"Fred, I shan't let you think of going out."

"Hold on." The double bell began to chirp.
They started up. Fred took the telephone.
"Hello, Meserve. You're there, then—! And your wife?
Good! Why I asked—she didn't seem to answer.
He says she went to let him in the barn.—
We're glad. Oh, say no more about it, man.
Drop in and see us when you're passing."

              "Well,
She has him then, though what she wants him for
I *don't* see."

          "Possibly not for herself.
Maybe she only wants him for the children."

"The whole to-do seems to have been for nothing.
What spoiled our night was to him just his fun.
What did he come in for?—To talk and visit?

Thought he'd just call to tell us it was snowing.
If he thinks he is goinIg to make our house
A halfway coffee house 'twixt town and nowhere——"

"I thought you'd feel you'd been too much concerned."

"You think you haven't been concerned yourself."

"If you mean he was inconsiderate
To rout us out to think for him at midnight
And then take our advice no more than nothing,
Why, I agree with you. But let's forgive him.
We've had a share in one night of his life.
What'll you bet he ever calls again?"

THE SOUND OF THE TREES

I wonder about the trees.
Why do we wish to bear
Forever the noise of these
More than another noise
So close to our dwelling place?
We suffer them by the day
Till we lose all measure of pace,
And fixity in our joys,
And acquire a listening air.
They are that that talks of going
But never gets away;
And that talks no less for knowing,
As it grows wiser and older,
That now it means to stay.
My feet tug at the floor
And my head sways to my shoulder
Sometimes when I watch trees sway,
From the window or the door.
I shall set forth for somewhere,
I shall make the reckless choice
Some day when they are in voice
And tossing so as to scare
The white clouds over them on.
I shall have less to say,
But I shall be gone.

NOTES

A BOY'S WILL

1. See Shakespeare, Sonnet 116: "But bears it out even to the edge of doom."
2. *fain to list:* glad to listen.
3. See the anonymous Scottish ballad "Waly, Waly": "I've locked my heart in a case o'goud, / And pinned it wi' a siller pin."
4. See Keats, "Ode to a Nightingale": "But being too happy in thine happiness."
5. *pogonias:* orchids.
6. *orchises:* orchids.
7. See Shakespeare, *The Tempest* (4.1.156–7): "We are such stuff / As dreams are made on."
8. *book of old-golden song:* an allusion to Frost's favorite book of poetry, *The Golden Treasury* (1861), edited by Francis Palgrave.
9. See Shakespeare, Sonnet 49: "And scarcely greet me with that sun, thine eye."
10. *fain to list:* glad to listen.
11. *swale:* a low, moist place in a tract of land.
12. See Keats, "Ode to a Nightingale": "With beaded bubbles winking at the brim."
13. *Demiurge:* creator of the world.
14. See Thomas D'Urfey, "Over the hills and far away."
15. See Marlowe, "The Passionate Shepherd to His Love": "Come live with me, and be my love."
16. See Joshua 10:13: "And the sun stood still, and the moon stayed."
17. *emulous:* jealous.
18. *wist:* know.

19. *offence:* pun on "a fence."
20. See Byron, "She Walks in Beauty."
21. See Virgil, "Eclogue, I": "longer shadows fall from the lofty mountain."
22. *Lunenburg:* a town in northern Vermont.
23. *Hor:* the mountain overlooking ancient Petra (in Jordan). Aaron the priest is said to have died on its summit (Numbers 20:22–29).
24. *Vermont Democrat:* Democrats are rare in Republican Vermont.
25. *Bill Taft:* William Howard Taft, American president, 1909–13.
26. *Gettysburg or Fredericksburg:* battles in the American Civil War.
27. *Garrison:* William Lloyd Garrison (1805–79), American journalist and abolitionist.
28. *Whittier:* James Greenleaf Whittier (1807–72), American poet.
29. *all men are . . . :* from the American Declaration of Independence (1776).
30. *the Welshman:* Thomas Jefferson (1743–1826), author of the Declaration of Independence, whose father had Welsh origins.
31. *the Creed:* the Apostles' Creed, the basic statement of the Christian faith.
32. *descended into Hades:* a reference to Christ in the Apostles' Creed.
33. *chewink:* finch.
34. See Genesis 10:25: "a servant of servants shall he be unto his brethren."
35. *Willoughby:* lake and summer resort in northern Vermont.
36. See Keats, "Ode to a Nightingale": "I cannot see what flowers are at my feet."
37. *Salem:* village in southeast New Hampshire.
38. *bulling:* bullying.
39. *Bow:* village in southeast New Hampshire.
40. See *Twelfth Night* (1.5.296–7): "What is your parentage?" "Above my fortunes, yet my state is well."
41. *Chicamoztoc:* myth of the pre-Columbian Aztec Indians of Mexico.
42. *Nausicaa:* a princess who discovered the shipwrecked Odysseus.
43. *dite:* bit.
44. See Matthew 5:13: "if the salt have lost his savour, wherewith shall it be salted?"
45. See *Macbeth* (1.1.1): "When shall we three meet again?"
46. *Langshang:* large Asiatic breed of poultry.
47. *Crystal Palace:* building designed by Sir Joseph Paxton and erected in Hyde Park, London, for the Great Exhibition in 1851.
48. *shooks:* a set of wooden parts, ready to be put together.

49. *Burroughs:* John Burroughs (1837–1921), American naturalist and writer.
50. *Cypripedium reginae:* Queen's orchid.
51. *sinus:* a small depression in a leaf.
52. See Matthew 24:27: "[Pilate] took water, and washed his hands before the multitude."
53. *clematis:* a flowering vine.
54. See Donne, "A Valediction: Forbidding Mourning": "'Twere profanation of our joys."

MOUNTAIN INTERVAL

The title refers to a tract of farm land located on a mountainside.

55. See Burns, "The Cotter's Saturday Night."
56. See Shakespeare, *Love's Labour's Lost* (5.2.922): "When icicles hang by the wall."
57. *hyla:* a tree frog.
58. See Keats, "Ode to a Nightingale": "To cease upon the midnight with no pain."
59. *Sirius:* the Dog Star, the brightest in the sky.
60. See Shelley, "Adonais": "Life, like a dome of many-coloured glass, / Stains the white radiance of Eternity."
61. *bracken:* thicket of ferns.
62. *trillium:* lilac-colored herb.
63. *pomace:* pulpy residue of apples.
64. *scurf:* shreds.
65. *range-finding:* coordinating gun sights and trajectories so bullets and shells can be fired accurately.
66. *mullein:* a weed.
67. *hepaticas:* herb of the buttercup family.
68. *brake:* thicket.
69. See Shakespeare, *As You Like It* (2.7.166): "Sans teeth, sans eyes, sans taste, sans everything."
70. *Grange:* farm association.
71. *Ile's / 'Bout out!:* the oil is about out.
72. *Racker Sect:* Frost invented this name.
73. *chickadee:* titmouse, a small bird with thick plumage and a short bill.
74. *the gift of tongues:* an outpouring of the spirit, as described in Acts 2:4, which enabled the Apostles to communicate in all foreign languages.

INDEX

ABOUT THE AUTHOR

Born in San Francisco and bred in New England, Robert Frost is considered one of the greatest poets of the twentieth century. He was a witty speaker, a brilliant reader of poetry, and a much-loved cultural icon. He won four Pulitzer Prizes and made cultural tours to South America, England, the Middle East, and Russia. His first three books, included in this volume, contain many of his most important poems.

ABOUT THE EDITOR

Jeffrey Meyers, a Fellow of the Royal Society of Literature, taught for thirty years in universities in America, England, and Japan. He has written and edited three books on biography, and published lives of Katherine Mansfield, Wyndham Lewis, Ernest Hemingway, Robert Lowell and his circle, D.H. Lawrence, Joseph Conrad, Edgar Allan Poe, F. Scott Fitzgerald, Edmund Wilson, and Robert Frost. He lives in Berkeley, California, and is now writing a life of Bogart.